Better Homes and Gardens®

CHRISTMAS COOKING
FROM THE HEART™

Great Gatherings

Meredith® Books
Des Moines, Iowa

Better Homes and Gardens®

CHRISTMAS COOKING
FROM THE HEART™

Test Kitchen

Our seal assures you that every recipe in *Christmas Cooking from the Heart*™ has been tested in the Better Homes and Gardens® Test Kitchen. This means that each recipe is practical and reliable, and meets our high standards of taste appeal. We guarantee your satisfaction with this book for as long as you own it.

All of us at Meredith® Consumer Marketing are dedicated to roviding you with information and ideas to enhance your home. We welcome your comments and suggestions. Write to us at: Meredith Consumer Marketing, 1716 Locust St., Des Moines, IA 50309-3023. *Christmas Cooking from the Heart* is available by mail. To order editions from past years, call 800/627-5490.

Cover Photography:
Front cover: White Chocolate Layer Cake with Cranberry Filling (page 80), Doubly Decadent Truffles (page 120), Tiamisu Biscotti (page 131), Easy Cocoa Fudge (page 118), Lemony Gingerbread People (page 129), Pralines (page 118), Pistachio-Lime Balls (page 100), Red Velvet Whoopie Pies with Peppermint Filling (page 107), Almond Apricot Windows (page 110), *Back cover:* Lemon-Berry Ribbon Torte (page 87)

MEREDITH CORPORATION CONSUMER MARKETING
Senior Vice President, Consumer Marketing: David Ball
Consumer Product Marketing Director: Steve Swanson
Consumer Product Marketing Manager: Wendy Merical
Business Director: Ron Clingman
Associate Director, Production: Douglas M. Johnston

WATERBURY PUBLICATIONS, INC.
Editorial Director: Lisa Kingsley
Creative Director: Ken Carlson
Associate Editor: Tricia Laning
Associate Design Director: Doug Samuelson
Graphic Designer: Kim Hopkins
Graphic Designer: Mindy Samuelson
Contributing Writer: Deborah Wagman
Contributing Copy Editor: Terri Fredrickson
Contributing Proofreaders: Gretchen Kauffman, Peg Smith
Contributing Indexer: Elizabeth T. Parson

BETTER HOMES AND GARDENS® MAGAZINE
Editor in Chief: Gayle Goodson Butler
Art Director: Michael D. Belknap
Deputy Editor, Food and Entertaining: Nancy Wall Hopkins
Senior Food Editor: Richard Swearinger
Associate Food Editor: Erin Simpson
Editorial Assistant: Renee Irey

MEREDITH PUBLISHING GROUP
President: Jack Griffin
Executive Vice President: Andy Sareyan
Vice President, Manufacturing: Bruce Heston

MEREDITH CORPORATION
President and Chief Executive Officer: Stephen M. Lacy

In Memoriam: E.T. Meredith III (1933–2003)

All of us at Meredith® Consumer Marketing are dedicated to providing you with information and ideas to enhance your home. We welcome your comments and suggestions. Write to us at: Meredith Consumer Marketing, 1716 Locust St., Des Moines, IA 50309-3023.

table of
contents

Raspberry and White Chocolate Brownies,
page 113

Baked Holiday Spiral Ham
with Raisin Sauce, page 12

great gatherings

Wherever there is true celebration, there is an abundance of wonderful food that draws friends and family together to enjoy one another's company and the familiar dishes and flavors that make the holiday season so special. *Christmas Cooking from the Heart* is full of fresh takes on traditional foods for celebrating every special occasion from Thanksgiving through New Year's. Each year, the culinary experts in the *Better Homes and Gardens®* Test Kitchen come up with new ways to enjoy favorite holiday recipes for appetizers, entrées, desserts, and edible gifts so you can plan an intimate Christmas Eve soup supper with the immediate family, a fabulous brunch for holiday houseguests, or bake a batch of cookies for coworkers. Everything you need to create a memorable holiday season is in this volume, including helpful hint and tips for planning, preparing, and organizing the busiest days of the year. Taking time to shop and cook in advance, so you can enjoy the celebration with family and friends, is the greatest gift you can give to yourself—and to those you love. Happy holidays!

Chocolate Flan,
page 94

Roasted Beets and Greens with Spicy
Orange Vinaigrette, page 26

Apricot-Glazed Ham Balls, page 41

the main event

This is the biggie—the meal that everyone waits for all year. Imagine gracing this season's holiday table with a ruby-glazed turkey, an herb-crusted beef rib roast, or a pork loin tumbled with autumnal fruits. Choose from a supporting cast of stupendous sides. The recipes on these pages will make those 365 days of anticipation well worth the wait.

Holiday Rib Roast, page 8

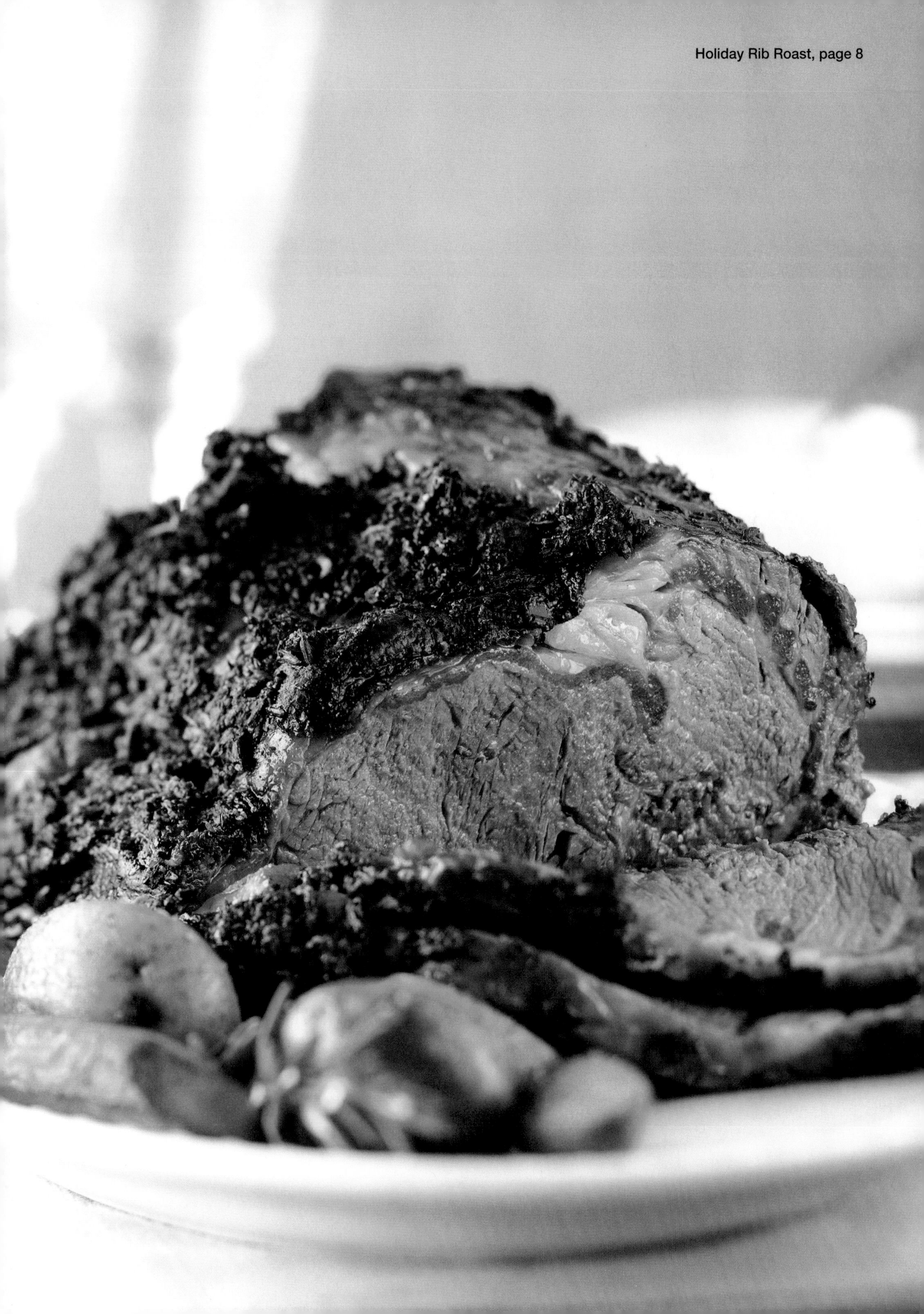

Holiday Rib Roast

2. In a small bowl combine garlic, herbes de Provence, 1 teaspoon salt, and pepper; mix well. Spread the 2 tablespoons mustard over beef; pat garlic mixture onto mustard. Insert an ovenproof thermometer into center of roast. The thermometer should not touch the bone.

3. Roast, uncovered, until desired doneness. Allow 1¾ to 2¼ hours for medium rare (135°F) or 2¼ to 2¾ hours for medium (150°F). Cover with foil; let stand for 15 minutes before carving. Temperature of the meat after standing should be 145°F for medium rare or 160°F for medium.

4. Meanwhile, in a small bowl stir together sour cream, ¼ cup mustard, the water, and ¼ teaspoon salt. Cover and chill until serving. Serve with beef.

Per serving: 688 cal., 44 g total fat (23 g sat. fat), 153 mg chol., 609 mg sodium, 2 g carbo., 0 g fiber, 44 g pro.

Holiday Rib Roast

Mouths will water when the aroma of herbes de Provence—a blend of basil, fennel, lavender, rosemary, sage, and thyme—wafts from your oven.

Prep: 20 minutes **Roast:** 1¾ hours
Stand: 15 minutes **Oven:** 350°F
Makes: 8 servings

- 1 **5- to 6-pound beef rib roast**
- 4 **cloves garlic, minced**
- 2 **teaspoons herbes de Provence**
- 1 **teaspoon salt**
- ½ **teaspoon black pepper**
- 2 **tablespoons horseradish mustard**
- 1 **8-ounce carton sour cream**
- ¼ **cup horseradish mustard**
- 2 **tablespoons water**
- ¼ **teaspoon salt**

1. Position oven rack just below center of oven. Preheat oven to 350°F. Place beef, fat side up, on a rack in a shallow roasting pan.

Rib Roast with Dijon-Sour Cream Sauce

The choice between bone-in or boneless rib roast is yours. When roasted on the bone, the beef will be more flavorful, but a boneless roast is easier to carve.

Prep: 25 minutes **Marinate:** 6 hours
Roast: 1¾ hours **Stand:** 15 minutes
Oven: 350°F **Makes:** 8 servings

- 1 **4-pound beef rib roast**
- ¾ **cup dry red wine**
- ¼ **cup lemon juice**
- 2 **teaspoons dried rosemary, crushed**
- 2 **teaspoons dried marjoram, crushed**
- ¼ **teaspoon garlic salt**
- 1 **recipe Dijon-Sour Cream Sauce**

1. Place meat in a large resealable plastic bag set in a shallow dish. For marinade, in a small bowl combine wine, lemon juice, rosemary, marjoram, and garlic salt. Pour over meat. Seal bag; turn to coat meat. Marinate in the refrigerator for at least 6 hours or up to 24 hours, turning bag occasionally. Drain meat, discarding marinade.

2. Preheat oven to 350°F. Place roast, fat side up, in an ungreased 9×13-inch baking pan or baking dish. Insert an oven-going meat thermometer into the center of the roast. The thermometer should not touch the bone.

3. Roast, uncovered, until desired doneness. Allow 1¾ to 2¼ hours for medium rare (135°F) or 2¼ to 2¾ hours for medium (150°F). Cover with foil; let stand 15 minutes. The temperature of the meat after standing should be 145°F for medium rare or 160°F for medium. Carve roast and serve with Dijon-Sour Cream Sauce.

Dijon-Sour Cream Sauce: In a small bowl stir together one 8-ounce carton sour cream, 2 tablespoons Dijon mustard, and ½ teaspoon lemon-pepper seasoning. Cover and chill until serving time.

Per serving: 274 cal., 15 g total fat (7 g sat. fat), 80 mg chol., 255 mg sodium, 2 g carbo., 0 g fiber, 30 g pro.

Honey-Ancho-Glazed Beef Tenderloin

Ancho chile powder is ground from dried Poblano chiles. It is the sweetest chile and provides great depth of flavor without excess heat.

Prep: 20 minutes **Soak:** 1 hour **Grill:** 35 minutes
Stand: 15 minutes **Makes:** 8 to 10 servings

- 2 **to 3 cups hickory wood chips**
- ½ **cup honey**
- 1 **tablespoon ground ancho chile pepper* or chili powder**
- ¼ **cup cooking oil**
- 1 **3- to 4-pound beef tenderloin**
- 1 **teaspoon salt**
- 1 **teaspoon black pepper**
     Watercress, key limes, kumquats, and/or tangerines wedges (optional)

1. At least 1 hour before grilling, soak wood chips in enough water to cover. Drain before using.

2. In a small saucepan combine honey and chile pepper. Cook and stir on medium-low heat until heated through. Remove from heat; stir in oil.

Brush some of the mixture over the beef tenderloin. Season beef with salt and black pepper.

3. In a grill with a cover arrange preheated coals around a drip pan. Test for medium heat above the drip pan. Sprinkle wood chips over coals. Pour 1 inch of water into the drip pan. Place roast on grill rack over the drip pan. Cover and grill for 35 to 45 minutes or until an instant-read thermometer inserted near the center of the roast registers 135°F, brushing with honey mixture occasionally during the first 20 minutes of grilling. Discard any remaining honey mixture.

4. Remove meat from grill. Cover and let stand for 15 minutes before slicing. (The temperature of the meat will rise 10°F during standing.) Transfer to a serving platter. If desired, garnish with watercress, key limes, kumquats, and tangerine wedges.

*Note: To grind ancho chile peppers, place dried, seeded, and stemmed ancho chile peppers in a blender. Cover and blend until ground.

Per serving: 325 cal., 17 g total fat (4 g sat. fat), 78 mg chol., 360 mg sodium, 18 g carbo., 0 g fiber, 27 g pro.

Honey-Ancho-Glazed
Beef Tenderloin

Pork Loin with Apples and Pears

Pears and apples have a special affinity for pork, and thry make this simple roasted loin party-perfect.

Prep: 25 minutes **Roast:** 65 minutes
Stand: 10 minutes **Oven:** 425°F **Makes:** 8 servings

- 2 **teaspoons black pepper**
- 1 **teaspoon salt**
- 1 **teaspoon garlic powder**
- 1 **3-pound boneless pork top loin roast (single loin)**
- ⅓ **cup molasses**
- 2 **tablespoons red wine vinegar**
- 1 **tablespoon reduced-sodium soy sauce**
- 1 **tablespoon olive oil**
- 3 **apples, cut in halves, wedges, or slices**
- 2 **red pears, cut in halves, wedges, or slices**
- 2 **tablespoons sugar**

1. Preheat oven to 425°F. Line a shallow roasting pan with heavy foil; lightly oil foil. Place meat rack in pan; set aside. In a small bowl combine pepper, salt, and garlic powder. Brush pork with oil; rub with pepper mixture. Place pork on rack in roasting pan. Roast, uncovered, for 35 minutes.

2. For glaze, in a skillet combine molasses, vinegar, and soy sauce. Bring to boiling. Reduce heat; simmer 1 minute. Transfer to a bowl. Set glaze and skillet aside.

3. Brush pork with glaze (reserve 2 tablespoons glaze for fruit). Roast 20 minutes more, brushing with glaze halfway through roasting. Roast another 10 minutes or until an instant-read thermometer inserted into the center of the roast registers 150°F. Remove from oven; cover with foil. Let stand 10 minutes before slicing.

Pork Loin with Apples and Pears

4. Meanwhile, in skillet used for glaze heat oil. Toss fruit with sugar. Add fruit to skillet; cover and cook 2 minutes. Uncover and cook 3 minutes more or until crisp-tender. Add reserved glaze; heat through. Serve pork with fruit and drizzle with pan juices.

Per serving: 361 cal., 10 g total fat (3 g sat. fat), 107 mg chol., 444 mg sodium, 28 g carbo., 3 g fiber, 39 g pro.

Currant-Glazed Roast Turkey

Glossy red currant glaze makes for a picture-perfect holiday bird. It may be hard to wait, but allowing the turkey to stand for 15 to 20 minutes guarantees moist and succulent slices.

Prep: 20 minutes **Roast:** 2¾ hours
Stand: 15 minutes **Oven:** 325°F
Makes: 8 to 10 servings

  1 **10- to 12-pound turkey**
  1 **tablespoon butter, melted**
  1 **recipe Currant Glaze**
  1 **recipe Pan Gravy (optional)**
  1 **recipe Herb Drizzle (optional)**
     Halved fresh plums, red seedless grapes, arugula, and/or fresh herb sprigs

1. Preheat oven to 325°F. Rinse the turkey body cavity; pat dry with paper towels. If desired, season body cavity with salt. Skewer turkey neck skin to back.

2. Tuck drumstick ends under the band of skin across the tail, if present. If there is no band of skin, tie the drumsticks securely to the tail. Twist wing tips under the back.

3. Place turkey, breast side up, on a rack in a shallow roasting pan. Brush with the butter. If desired, insert a meat thermometer into the center of an inside thigh muscle. The thermometer should not touch bone. Cover turkey loosely with foil.

4. Roast for 2¾ to 3 hours. During the last 45 minutes of roasting, remove foil and cut band of skin or string between drumsticks so thighs cook evenly. During the last 15 minutes of roasting, brush twice with the Currant Glaze. Continue roasting until the thermometer registers 180°F. (The juices should run clear and drumsticks should move easily in their sockets.)

5. Remove turkey from oven. Let stand for 15 to 20 minutes before carving. Garnish platter with plums, grapes, arugula, and/or herb sprigs. Carve turkey. If desired, serve with Pan Gravy and/or Herb Drizzle.

Currant Glaze: In a small saucepan combine ½ cup red currant or plum jelly, 1 tablespoon lemon juice, 1 teaspoon dry mustard, 1 teaspoon Worcestershire sauce, and ¼ teaspoon black pepper. Heat and stir until jelly is melted.

Per serving: 280 cal., 8 g total fat (3 g sat. fat), 154 mg chol., 93 mg sodium, 7 g carbo., 0 g fiber, 42 g pro.

Pan Gravy: While turkey stands after roasting, pour pan drippings into a large measuring cup. Scrape the browned bits from the pan into the cup. Skim and reserve fat from the drippings. Heat ¼ cup of the fat in a medium saucepan (discard any remaining fat). Cook and stir ¼ cup minced shallot or finely chopped onion in the fat until tender. Stir in ¼ cup all-purpose flour. Add enough chicken broth to remaining drippings in the measuring cup to equal 2 cups; add broth mixture all at once to flour mixture in saucepan. Cook and stir on medium heat until thickened and bubbly. Cook and stir for 1 minute more. Season to taste with salt and black pepper.

Herb Drizzle: In a saucepan melt 2 tablespoons butter; stir in 1 tablespoon cornstarch and ¼ teaspoon cracked black pepper. Add 1⅓ cups reduced-sodium chicken broth. Cook and stir until thickened and bubbly. Stir in 2 teaspoons snipped fresh thyme and 1 teaspoon snipped fresh rosemary. Cook and stir 1 to 2 minutes more.

Baked Holiday Spiral Ham
with Raisin Sauce

Baked Holiday Spiral Ham with Raisin Sauce

Roasting ham on a rack will allow the entire exterior of the ham to become beautifully caramelized, crusty, and scrumptious.

Prep: 15 minutes **Roast:** 1¾ hours **Oven:** 325°F
Makes: 12 to 14 servings

1	4- to 5-pound cooked boneless spiral-sliced honey-cured ham
3	cups brown sauce or brown gravy*
¼	cup packed brown sugar
2	tablespoons frozen orange juice concentrate
1	tablespoon lemon juice
1	tablespoon cider vinegar
⅔	cup golden raisins or raisins

1. Preheat oven to 325°F. Place ham on a rack in a shallow roasting pan. Insert an oven-going thermometer into center of ham. Bake, covered with foil, for 1¾ to 2¼ hours or until thermometer registers 140°F.

2. For sauce, in a medium saucepan combine brown sauce, brown sugar, orange juice concentrate, lemon juice, and vinegar. Bring to boiling, stirring constantly. Stir in raisins; heat through. Remove from heat.

3. To serve, slice ham. Pass warm brown sauce.

*For brown sauce:** Prepare enough brown sauce mix or brown gravy mix to make 3 cups.

Per serving: 349 cal., 17 g total fat (5 g sat. fat), 86 mg chol., 2,415 mg sodium, 21 g carbo., 1 g fiber, 27 g pro.

Wild Mushroom Gravy

Packets of magnificent dried mushrooms are usuallly located in supermarket produce sections, shelved alongside specialty products such as dried fruits, pumpkin seeds, and sugarcane skewers.

Prep: 20 minutes **Stand:** 30 minutes
Makes: 2½ cups or 9 servings

- ¼ cup dried mushrooms (such as shiitakes, porcini, oyster mushrooms, and/or chanterelles)
- 1 cup boiling water
- 1 cup sliced fresh mushrooms
- ½ cup chopped onion (1 medium)
- 2 tablespoons butter
- ¼ cup all-purpose flour
- 1 cup chicken broth
- ½ teaspoon salt
- ¼ teaspoon freshly ground black pepper
- 2 teaspoons snipped fresh marjoram, thyme, or oregano or ½ teaspoon dried marjoram, thyme, or oregano, crushed
  Salt (optional)
  Freshly ground black pepper (optional)

1. Place dried mushrooms in a small bowl. Pour the boiling water over dried mushrooms. Let stand for 30 minutes. Drain mushrooms, reserving liquid. Strain the liquid through a fine-mesh sieve lined with 100%-cotton cheesecloth; set liquid aside. Rinse and drain mushrooms a second time, discarding rinse water. Set mushrooms aside.

2. Meanwhile, in a medium saucepan cook fresh mushrooms and chopped onion in hot butter until mushrooms are tender. Stir in flour. Add reserved mushroom liquid, broth, salt, pepper, and, if using, dried herb. Cook and stir on medium heat until thickened and bubbly; cook and stir for 1 minute more. Stir in soaked mushrooms and, if using, fresh herb. If desired, season gravy to taste with additional salt and freshly ground black pepper. Pour gravy into a gravy boat or bowl.

Per ¼ cup: 46 cal., 3 g total fat (2 g sat. fat)), 7 mg chol., 243 mg sodium, 5 g carbo., 0 g fiber, 1 g pro.

Madeira Gravy

Madeira—a Portuguese wine—ranges from quite dry to relatively sweet. For best flavor, choose a Madeira on the drier side, such as Sercial.

Start to Finish: 20 minutes
Makes: 4 cups or 16 servings

- Pan drippings from roasted turkey or chicken
  Chicken broth (optional)
- ⅓ cup all-purpose flour
- 3 cups chicken broth
- ⅓ cup Madeira wine
- ⅛ teaspoon freshly ground black pepper

1. Pour pan drippings into a fat separator or into a large glass measuring cup. If using a fat separator, pour off fat into a glass measuring cup. (If using a large measuring cup, use a spoon to skim and reserve fat from drippings.) Pour ¼ cup of the fat into the roasting pan; discard remaining fat. Measure drippings. If necessary, add chicken broth to remaining drippings to equal ¾ cup liquid; set aside.

2. Set roasting pan on the stovetop. Stir flour into fat in roasting pan until smooth. Cook and stir on medium heat for 1 to 2 minutes or until lightly browned.

3. Gradually whisk in the ¾ cup pan drippings, the 3 cups broth, the Madeira, and pepper. Bring to boiling; reduce heat to medium-low, whisking gravy until smooth. Simmer, uncovered, for 2 minutes, stirring occasionally. Pour gravy through a fine-mesh sieve into a gravy boat or bowl.

Per ¼ cup: 50 cal., 4 g total fat (1 g sat. fat), 3 mg chol., 235 mg sodium, 2 g carbo., 0 g fiber, 1 g pro.

Fresh Cranberry-Fig Relish

This rosy relish is superalative with turkey, and fantastic with grilled pork. Pop an extra bag of cranberries in the freezer to save for summertime use.

Prep: 10 minutes **Chill:** 2 hours
Makes: 4 cups or 16 servings

- 4 cups fresh or frozen cranberries
- 1 cup dried figs, stems removed
- 2 tablespoons snipped fresh mint leaves
- 1 cup orange marmalade
- 2 tablespoons balsamic vinegar

1. Using a food processor or handheld food chopper, process or chop cranberries and dried figs until coarsely chopped. Transfer to bowl; add mint. In a small bowl stir together marmalade and balsamic vinegar. Add to cranberry mixture; stir well. Cover and refrigerate for at least 2 hours.

***Note:** If cranberries are frozen, measure while frozen. Let stand at room temperature about 15 minutes to thaw slightly before processing.

Per serving: 96 cal., 0 g total fat, 0 mg chol., 13 mg sodium, 25 g carbo., 3 g fiber, 1 g pro.

Cranberry-Apple-Orange Relish

Choose Granny Smith, Rome, or Winesap apples to imbue this concoction with appealing zestiness.

Prep: 20 minutes **Chill:** 2 hours
Makes: 3 cups or 12 servings

- 2 medium tart apples, cored
- 1½ cups fresh cranberries
- 1 small navel orange, peeled
- ¼ cup pecan pieces
- ⅓ to ½ cup sugar
   Finely shredded orange peel (optional)
   Fresh cranberries (optional)

1. Using a food processor or food grinder with a coarse blade, coarsely chop apples, cranberries, oranges, and pecans in batches to about ¼-inch pieces.

2. In a large bowl combine fruit mixture and sugar. Cover and refrigerate for 2 hours. Stir before serving. If desired, garnish with orange peel and fresh cranberries.

Per serving: 63 cal., 2 g total fat (0 g sat. fat), 0 mg chol., 1 g sodium, 13 g carbo., 2 g fiber, 0 g pro.

Cherry-Pomegranate Chutney

If you have difficulty finding unsweetened pomegranate juice at your supermarket, stop by a health food store.

Prep: 15 minutes **Cook:** 30 minutes
Makes: 1¾ cups or 14 servings

- 1 tablespoon olive oil
- 1 cup chopped onions (2 medium)
- 1 tablespoon grated fresh ginger
- 1 teaspoon minced garlic
- ¼ teaspoon ground cinnamon
- ⅛ teaspoon ground allspice
- 1 12-ounce package frozen dark sweet cherries
- ½ cup unsweetened pomegranate juice
- 3 tablespoons sugar
- ¾ cup pomegranate seeds (1 small)
- ¼ teaspoon salt

1. In large nonstick skillet heat oil on medium heat. Add onions, ginger, and garlic. Cook for 5 to 6 minutes or until tender and translucent, stirring occasionally. Add cinnamon and allspice; cook and stir about 15 to 20 seconds. Add cherries, pomegranate juice, and sugar.

2. Increase heat to medium-high. Bring onion-cherry mixture to boiling. Reduce heat to medium-low. Simmer, uncovered, for 30 minutes or until onion-cherry mixture is thickened, stirring occasionally. Remove from heat. Stir in pomegranate seeds and salt. Refrigerate chutney, covered, up to 1 week.

Per 2 tablespoons: 54 cal., 1 g total fat (0 g sat. fat), 0 mg chol., 43 mg sodium, 11 g carbo., 1 g fiber, 1 g pro.

Pear-Pecan Stuffing

To keep a closer eye on toasting pecans, skip the oven. Instead, place nuts in a large dry skillet and shake them over medium heat until fragrant.

Prep: 30 minutes **Bake:** 40 minutes **Oven:** 350°F
Makes: about 12 to 14 servings

- 1 pound firm-textured white sandwich bread
- 2 large firm ripe Bartlett pears, cored, peeled, and chopped
- 1 large onion, chopped (1 cup)
- 2 tablespoons butter (no substitutes)
- ½ to ¾ cup water
- ¼ cup butter (no substitutes)
- 1 cup pecan halves, toasted and coarsely chopped
- 2 tablespoons snipped fresh parsley
- ¼ teaspoon freshly grated nutmeg
- ⅛ teaspoon salt
  Dash freshly ground black pepper

1. Preheat oven to 350°F. To dry the bread, spread the slices on baking sheets. Bake about 20 minutes or until bread is dry.

2. In a large skillet cook pears and onion in 2 tablespoons hot butter on medium-high heat about 4 minutes or until pears and onion are tender, stirring occasionally. Set aside.

3. For stuffing, break dried bread into small pieces; place in an extra-large bowl. In a small saucepan combine ½ cup of the water and the ¼ cup butter. Bring to boiling. Drizzle butter mixture over bread pieces; toss gently to combine. Stir in pear mixture, pecans, parsley, nutmeg, salt, and pepper. Drizzle stuffing with enough of the remaining ¼ cup water to moisten; toss lightly to combine.

4. Transfer stuffing to a 2½- to 3-quart casserole.* Bake, covered, alongside turkey about 40 minutes or until heated through.

*Note: Or use to stuff one 10- to 12-pound turkey.

Per serving: 244 cal., 15 g total fat (4 g sat. fat), 16 mg chol., 291 mg sodium, 26 g carbo., 2 g fiber, 4 g pro.

Wild Rice Stuffing

Fennel's fragrant, graceful greenery makes a gorgeous garnish—be sure to save it.

Prep: 55 minutes **Bake:** 30 minutes **Oven:** 325°F
Makes: 18 servings

- 1 **cup uncooked wild rice**
- 3 **cups water**
- ½ **cup uncooked long grain rice**
- 1 **pound bulk Italian sausage or bulk pork sausage**
- 1 **tablespoon olive oil**
- 3 **cups chopped onions (3 large)**
- 2 **cups chopped fennel**
- 8 **ounces fresh cremini, shiitake, or button mushrooms, quartered**
- ¾ **teaspoon salt**
- ½ **teaspoon freshly ground black pepper**
- 1 **cup dried tart red cherries or dried cranberries**
- ½ **cup snipped fresh parsley**

1. In a medium bowl soak wild rice in cold water; discard grains that float to the top. Drain wild rice. In a large saucepan bring the 3 cups water to boiling; add uncooked wild rice. Return to boiling; reduce heat. Cover and simmer for 25 minutes. Add uncooked long grain rice. Cover and simmer about 20 minutes more or until rice is tender and most liquid is absorbed. Remove from heat.

2. Preheat oven to 325°F. Grease a 3-quart rectangular baking dish; set aside. In a very large skillet cook sausage in hot oil about 5 minutes or until brown. Using a slotted spoon, transfer sausage to a very large bowl; reserve 1 tablespoon of the drippings in skillet (add additional oil, if necessary). Add onions, fennel, mushrooms, salt, and pepper; cook about 5 minutes or until vegetables are tender, stirring occasionally. Stir in cherries; cook for 2 minutes more. Remove from heat. Add onion mixture and cooked rice mixture to sausage in bowl; stir to combine.

3. Spoon stuffing into prepared baking dish. Bake, covered, for 30 to 35 minutes or until heated through. Stir in parsley before serving.

Per serving: 168 cal., 7 g total fat (2 g sat. fat), 17 mg chol., 245 mg sodium, 20 g carbo., 4 g fiber, 6 g pro.

Roasted Chestnut and Andouille Sausage Stuffing

Spicy, smoky andouille [ahn-DOO-ee] sausage is one of the Cajun culture's greatest contributions to the world of good tastes.

Prep: 30 minutes **Bake:** 30 minutes **Oven:** 325°F
Makes: 8 cups or 16 servings

- 1 **10-ounce can whole, peeled chestnuts, drained**
- 8 **ounces cooked andouille or smoked sausage, chopped**
- 3 **cups soft bread crumbs**
- 3 **cups crumbled corn bread**
- 2 **tablespoons snipped fresh parsley**
- 1 **tablespoon snipped fresh thyme**
- ½ **teaspoon salt**
- ¼ to ½ **teaspoon black pepper**
- ¼ **cup butter**
- ½ **cup finely chopped shallots**
- ¼ to ½ **cup water**

1. Place chestnuts in a very large bowl. Coarsely mash with a potato masher. Stir in cooked sausage, bread crumbs, corn bread, parsley, thyme, salt, and pepper; set aside.

2. In a small skillet melt butter on medium heat. Add shallots. Cook for 4 to 5 minutes or until tender, stirring occasionally. Add shallot mixture to chestnut mixture; toss to combine. Add water to desired moistness.

3. Use to stuff a whole broiler-fryer chicken, turkey, or pork chops. Place extra stuffing in a casserole. Bake, covered, alongside meat or poultry for 30 to 45 minutes or until heated through.

Per serving: 116 cal., 5 g total fat (2 g sat. fat), 24 mg chol., 324 mg sodium, 14 g carbo., 0 g fiber, 5 g pro.

Autumn Vegetable Pilaf

Vinegar may seem like an odd ingredient in a rice dish, but it provides an incredible counterpoint to the vegetables' sweetness.

Prep: 15 minutes **Roast:** 15 minutes
Oven: 400°F **Makes:** 6 servings

- 1 6- to 7.2-ounce package rice pilaf mix
- 2 tablespoons olive oil
- 2 cloves garlic, minced
- 1 teaspoon dried thyme, crushed
- 1 large sweet potato or carrot, peeled and cut into ½-inch cubes
- 1 medium zucchini, halved lengthwise and cut into ½-inch pieces
- 1 small red onion, cut into wedges
- ⅓ cup chopped pecans or walnuts, toasted
- 1 tablespoon cider vinegar

1. Preheat oven to 400°F. Cook rice mix according to package directions, except omit butter or oil.

2. Meanwhile, in a large bowl stir together the oil, garlic, and thyme. Add sweet potato, zucchini, and onion, stirring to coat. Spread vegetables in a single layer in a 15×10×1-inch baking pan. Roast, uncovered, for 15 to 20 minutes or until vegetables are lightly browned and tender, stirring occasionally.

3. Stir roasted vegetables, nuts, and vinegar into hot rice pilaf.

Per serving: 244 cal., 9 g total fat (1 g sat. fat), 0 mg chol., 349 mg sodium, 37 g carbo., 4 g fiber, 4 g pro.

Creamy Brussels Sprouts
with Peppered Bacon

until liquid is almost evaporated. Add cream. Cook
4 minutes more or until thickened.

3. Transfer sprouts to serving dish. Sprinkle with
crumbled bacon and cracked pepper.

Per serving: 174 cal., 14 g total fat (7 g sat. fat), 38 mg chol., 305 mg
sodium, 10 g carbo., 4 g fiber, 6 g pro.

Rice-Vermicelli Pilaf

*This perfect pilaf will remind you of that famous box
mix called the "San Fransisco treat," but it's leaps and
bounds more delicious.*

Prep: 10 minutes Cook: 20 minutes
Makes: 4 servings

- 1   cup long grain white rice
- ½   cup finely broken (½- to ¾-inch pieces)
      dried angel hair pasta (3 ounces)*
- ⅓   cup finely chopped onion
- 3   tablespoons butter
- 1   14-ounce can chicken or beef broth
- ¼   cup water
- ¼   teaspoon salt
- ¼   teaspoon black pepper
      Snipped fresh basil, dill, and/or crumbled
      crisp-cooked bacon or pancetta

1. In a medium saucepan cook rice, broken angel
hair pasta, and onion in hot butter on medium heat
for 4 to 5 minutes or until pasta is lightly browned
and onion is nearly tender. Carefully add broth,
water, salt, and pepper; bring to boiling. Reduce
heat. Simmer, covered, for 15 to 20 minutes or
until the rice is tender and broth is absorbed. Fluff
rice with a fork. Sprinkle with basil before serving.

*Note: To finely break the angel hair pasta, place
ther pasta in a heavy-duty resealable plastic bag set
in a bowl. Then use your hands to break the pasta
into short lengths. Use the bottom of a can of food
to crush the pasta into very short lengths, about
½ inch long.

Per serving: 336 cal., 9 g total fat (6 g sat. fat), 24 mg chol., 607 mg sodium,
55 g carbo., 1 g fiber, 7 g pro.

Creamy Brussels Sprouts with Peppered Bacon

*This recipe will catapult Brussels sprouts to the top of
your family's list of favorite vegetables.*

Prep: 20 minutes Cook: 15 minutes
Makes: 8 servings

- 4   slices peppered bacon
- 2   pounds Brussels sprouts, trimmed and
      halved through stem ends
- ¾   cup reduced-sodium chicken broth
- ½   teaspoon kosher salt
- ¼   teaspoon freshly ground black pepper
- ¾   cup whipping cream
      Cracked black pepper

1. In a large skillet cook bacon on medium heat
until browned and crisp. Drain on paper towels,
reserving 2 tablespoons drippings in skillet.
Crumble bacon; set aside.

2. Add Brussels sprouts to drippings in skillet.
Cook on medium heat 4 minutes, stirring
occasionally. Add broth, salt, and pepper. Heat
to boiling. Reduce heat. Simmer, covered, for
5 minutes. Uncover; cook 2 to 4 minutes more or

Spiced Parsnips with Toasted Coconut

Parsnips are often protected by a layer of thick parafin wax. The coating— intended to keep the roots from drying out—is easily removed with a vegetable peeler.

Prep: 25 minutes **Cook:** 12 minutes
Makes: 10 servings

  2 **pounds parsnips, peeled and sliced ½ inch thick (about 8 medium)**
  1 **pound sweet potatoes (about 2 medium), peeled and sliced ½ inch thick**
  ⅔ **cup whipping cream**
  ¼ **cup butter, softened**
  1 **tablespoon mild-flavor molasses**
  ½ **teaspoon salt**
  ½ **teaspoon ground cinnamon**
  ¼ **teaspoon ground ginger**
  ¼ **teaspoon black pepper**
  ½ **cup shredded coconut, toasted**

1. In a Dutch oven cook parsnips and sweet potatoes, covered, in a small amount of boiling water for 12 to 15 minutes or until very tender; drain and return to Dutch oven. Add whipping cream, butter, molasses, salt, cinnamon, ginger, and pepper. Mash with a potato masher or beat with an electric mixer on low speed. Reheat, if needed. To serve, sprinkle with coconut.

Per serving: 216 cal., 13 g total fat (8 g sat. fat), 34 mg chol., 197 mg sodium, 25 g carbo., 5 g fiber, 2 g pro.

Roasted Kale and Red Onions

When purchasing kale, choose small bunches and avoid those with limp or yellowing leaves.

Prep: 35 minutes **Cook:** 20 minutes **Oven:** 375°F
Makes: 8 servings

  3 **large red onions, cut in wedges**
  6 **tablespoons olive oil, divided**
  ¾ **teaspoon salt**
  ½ **teaspoon black pepper**
  ½ **cup chicken broth**
  3 **tablespooons balsamic vinegar**
  1 **tablespoon butter**
  2 **bunches (about 1¼ pounds) kale, stems removed and coarsely chopped**
  2 **cloves garlic, minced**

1. Preheat oven to 375°F. Line a large roasting pan with foil; set aside. In a large bowl toss onions with 1 tablespoon of the oil, ¼ teaspoon of the salt, and ¼ teaspoon of the pepper; set aside.

2. Heat 1 tablespoon of the oil in a large skillet; add onion mixture. Cook on medium-high heat 5 minutes, stirring occasionally, until onions begin to brown. Reduce heat to medium-low. Add broth and vinegar. Cover and cook 15 minutes or until onions are tender. Add butter. Increase heat to high; cook 2 to 3 minutes more, shaking pan occasionally, until onions are glazed.

3. Meanwhile, add kale to roasting pan. Toss with remaining oil, garlic, salt, and pepper. Roast, uncovered, 15 minutes, tossing 3 times. To serve, gently toss with onions.

Per serving: 150 cal., 12 g total fat (2 g sat. fat), 4 mg chol., 310 mg sodium, 10 g carbo., 1 g fiber, 2 g pro.

Roasted Kale and Red Onions

Braised Fennel with Dill

Although fennel is as common as carrots in Mediterreanean cuisine, it is relatively new to the American market. Give it a try—its subtle licorice flavor will win you over.

Prep: 10 minutes **Cook:** 30 minutes
Makes: 6 servings

- 3 **medium fennel bulbs**
- 2 **tablespoons butter**
- ½ **cup chicken broth**
- ¼ **cup dry white wine**
- ¼ **teaspoon salt**
- ⅛ **to ¼ teaspoon black pepper**
- 3 **tablespoons snipped fresh dill**

1. Cut off and discard fennel stalks. Remove any wilted outer layers and cut a thin slice from the base of each bulb. Wash bulbs and cut them in half lengthwise. Cut fennel into 1-inch wedges.

2. In a large skillet melt butter on medium heat. Add fennel wedges, chicken broth, wine, salt, and pepper. Cover and cook 20 minutes or until fennel is tender, stirring occasionally. Cook, uncovered, 10 minutes more or until edges of fennel are lightly browned and liquid is evaporated. Stir in dill.

Per serving: 80 cal., 4 g total fat (2 g sat. fat), 10 mg chol., 266 mg sodium, 9 g carbo., 4 g fiber, 2 g pro.

Spiced Honey-Roasted Cauliflower

The combination of golden-sweet honey and salty-savory mustard takes cauliflower to a scrumptious new level.

Prep: 20 minutes **Roast:** 25 minutes
Oven: 350° F/400° F **Makes:** 8 servings

- ½ **cup honey**
- ¼ **cup whole grain mustard**
- ¼ **cup butter, softened**
- ½ **cup fresh bread crumbs**
- ⅓ **cup chopped fresh herbs (such as basil, parsley, and thyme)**
- 2 **heads cauliflower, trimmed and cleaned (7 cups)**
  Coarsely chopped fresh herbs (such as basil, parsley, and thyme)

1. Preheat oven to 350°F. In a small bowl combine the honey, mustard, butter, bread crumbs, and the ⅓ cup of the herbs. Set aside.

2. Place cauliflower, stem sides down, in a deep baking dish large enough to hold both heads. Add about ¼ inch of hot water to the dish. Cover with foil. Bake 8 to 10 minutes or until the water begins to steam. Remove foil. Carefully pour off water. Return cauliflower to oven. Increase oven temperature to 400°F. Bake for 5 minutes to dry the heads. Remove from oven and coat well with the bread crumb mixture. Return to oven. Roast 12 to 15 minutes more or until the cauliflower heads are well browned. To serve, sprinkle with additional chopped fresh herbs.

Per serving: 158 cal., 6 g total fat (4 g sat. fat), 15 mg chol., 275 mg sodium, 25 g carbo., 3 g fiber, 3 g pro.

Skillet-Browned Broccoli with Pan-Toasted Garlic

This healthful vegetable dish is sure to bring out your inner Italian.

Prep: 15 minutes **Cook:** 15 minutes
Makes: 8 servings

- 3 **large broccoli stems with stem end attached**
- ¼ **cup extra virgin olive oil**
  Coarse sea salt
  Freshly ground black pepper
- 3 **tablespoons thinly sliced garlic cloves**

1. Preheat a large cast-iron skillet on medium heat. Slice broccoli heads lengthwise into 1-inch-thick slices, cutting from the bottom of the stems through the crown to preserve the shape of the broccoli (reserve any florets that fall away for another use). Brush both sides of each broccoli slice with some of the olive oil and sprinkle lightly with salt and pepper.

2. Place half of the slices in the heated skillet and set a heavy medium skillet on the slices to press them to the cast-iron skillet. Cook over medium heat for 3 to 4 minutes or until well-browned. Turn slices and cook second side for 3 to 4 minutes more or until browned (for more tender broccoli, cook over medium-low heat for 5 to 6 minutes per side). Repeat with remaining broccoli slices. Transfer to a warm platter, cover, and keep warm in a 300°F oven or cover with foil while cooking the remaining broccoli.

3. Drizzle remaining olive oil into the hot skillet, reduce heat to medium-low and add garlic slices. Cook garlic for 2 minutes or until the slices are lightly browned, stirring constantly. Transfer to a plate lined with paper towels and sprinkle lightly with salt and pepper.

4. Arrange broccoli on serving platter. Sprinkle toasted garlic slices over broccoli.

Per serving: 84 cal., 7 g total fat (1 g sat. fat), 0 mg chol., 119 mg sodium, 5 g carbo., 2 g fiber, 2 g pro.

Spiced Honey-Roasted Cauliflower

Skillet-Browned Broccoli with Pan-Toasted Garlic

Spinach-Pea Risotto

Italian-grown Arborio rice is a short-grain variety. Its high starch content is responsible for the risotto's luxuriously creamy texture.

Start to Finish: 40 minutes **Makes:** 6 servings

- 2 **cloves garlic, minced**
- 2 **tablespoons olive oil**
- 1 **cup Arborio rice**
- ½ **cup thinly sliced carrot (1)**
- 2 **14-ounce cans vegetable broth or reduced-sodium chicken broth (3½ cups)**
- 2 **cups fresh spinach leaves, coarsely chopped**
- 1 **cup frozen baby or regular peas**
- 2 **ounces Parmigiano-Reggiano cheese, shredded**
- ⅓ **cup thinly sliced green onions (3)**
- ¼ **cup thin wedges fresh radishes**
- 2 **teaspoons snipped fresh tarragon Parmigiano-Reggiano cheese shards**

1. In a 3-quart saucepan cook garlic in hot oil on medium heat for 30 seconds. Add the rice. Cook about 5 minutes or until rice is golden brown, stirring frequently. Remove from heat. Stir in carrot.

2. Meanwhile, in a 1½-quart saucepan bring broth to boiling. Reduce heat and simmer.

3. Carefully stir 1 cup hot broth into rice mixture. Cook over medium heat until liquid is absorbed, stirring frequently. Add ½ cup broth at a time, stirring frequently until broth is absorbed before adding more broth (about 22 minutes).

4. Stir in any remaining broth. Cook and stir just until rice is tender and creamy. Stir in spinach, peas, shredded cheese, green onions, radishes, and tarragon; heat through. Top with cheese shards. Serve immediately.

Per serving: 191 cal., 7 g total fat (2 g sat. fat), 7 mg chol., 723 mg sodium, 25 g carbo., 2 g fiber, 7 g pro.

Shortcut Classic Risotto: Prepare as above through Step 1, except reduce broth to 3 cups. Carefully stir in all of the broth. Bring to boiling; reduce heat. Cover, simmer for 20 minutes (do not lift cover). Remove from heat. Stir in spinach, peas, cheese, green onions, radishes, and tarragon. Cover; let stand for 5 minutes. Rice should just be tender and mixture should be slightly creamy. Serve immediately. If desired, garnish with cheese shards.

Mashed Sweet Potatoes with White Cheddar

This superlative side dish is one you can feel especially good about serving. It's lick-the-plate yummy and packed with vitamins A and C.

Prep: 40 minutes **Bake:** 70 minutes
Cook: 5 minutes **Oven:** 425°F/325°F
Makes: 8 servings

- 3 **pounds sweet potatoes (about 7 medium)**
- ¼ **cup butter**
- 1 **teaspoon kosher salt or salt**
- 3 **ounces white cheddar cheese, shredded**
- ¼ **cup bourbon or orange juice**
- ¼ **cup whipping cream**
- ¼ **cup packed dark brown sugar**

Spinach-Pea Risotto

1 **large red onion, cut into thin wedges**
2 **medium red apples, cored and cut into wedges**
2 **teaspoons snipped fresh thyme**
¼ **teaspoon black pepper**

1. Preheat oven to 425°F. Scrub potatoes and prick with fork; place on foil-lined baking sheet. Bake 40 minutes or until tender. Reduce oven to 325°F.

2. When potatoes are cool enough to handle, halve and scrape pulp from skin. Transfer to bowl. Mash with 2 tablespoons of the butter, and ¾ teaspoon of the salt. Stir in cheese, bourbon, cream, and 2 tablespoons of the brown sugar. Transfer to a buttered 1½-quart casserole. Cover; bake 30 minutes or until heated through.

3. Meanwhile, in microwave-safe 2-quart casserole combine remaining butter, the remaining ¼ teaspoon salt, and brown sugar; add onion. Microwave, uncovered, on high for 3 to 4 minutes or until onion is crisp-tender; add apples. Cover and cook 2 minutes more or until apples are tender. Stir in thyme and pepper. Serve with sweet potatoes.

Per serving: 293 cal., 12 g total fat (8 g sat. fat), 37 mg chol., 421 mg sodium, 38 g carbo., 5 g fiber, 5 g pro.

½ **teaspoon salt**
½ **teaspoon black pepper**
½ **teaspoon finely shredded orange peel**
2 **tablespoons snipped fresh parsley**
2 **tablespoons thinly sliced green onion (1)**
2 **tablespoons snipped dried tomatoes (not oil-packed)**
2 **tablespoons sliced almonds, toasted (see note, page 24)**

1. Preheat oven to 375°F. Place squash in a large shallow baking pan. Drizzle with 1 tablespoon of the oil and sprinkle with salt. Bake, uncovered, for 20 minutes. Add cauliflower, broccoli, and sweet pepper; toss to coat. Bake, uncovered, 20 to 25 minutes more or until vegetables are tender.

2. In a bowl whisk together the remaining 2 tablespoons oil, lemon juice, orange juice concentrate, garlic, the ½ teaspoon salt, black pepper, and orange peel. In another bowl stir together parsley, green onion, tomatoes, and almonds. Add lemon juice mixture; toss to coat. Transfer to serving dish; sprinkle with parsley mixture.

Per ¾ cup: 116 cal., 6 g total fat (1 g sat. fat), 0 mg chol., 327 mg sodium, 15 g carbo., 3 g fiber, 3 g pro.

Roasted Vegetables Gremolata

Move over greeen bean casserole. Make room for this colorful celebration of flavors.

Prep: 25 minutes **Bake:** 40 minutes
Makes: 8 to 10 servings **Oven:** 375°F

1 **medium butternut squash, peeled, seeded, and cut into ½-inch pieces**
3 **tablespoons olive oil**
½ **of a medium head cauliflower, trimmed and cut into ½-inch slices (1¾ cups)**
½ **of a medium bunch broccoli, trimmed and cut into ½-inch slices (1½ cups)**
1 **cup red sweet pepper, seeded and cut into bite-size strips (1 large)**
2 **tablespoons lemon juice**
2 **tablespoons frozen orange juice concentrate, thawed**
1 **large clove garlic, minced**

Green Beans with Lime

In American grocery stores, hazelnuts are often called filberts.

Prep: 15 minutes **Cook:** 6 minutes
Makes: 8 servings

- 2 **pounds fresh green beans, trimmed**
- ⅓ **cup snipped fresh parsley**
- 1 **tablespoon snipped fresh rosemary**
- 2 **teaspoons finely shredded lime peel**
- 1 **tablespoon fresh lime juice**
- ½ **teaspoon minced garlic**
- 2 **tablespoons extra virgin olive oil**
- ⅓ **cup hazelnuts, toasted and chopped***
  Lime wedges (optional)

Green Beans with Lime

1. Bring a large saucepan of water to boiling. Add 1 tablespoon salt and green beans. Cook beans until crisp-tender, 3 to 4 minutes. Drain and immediately plunge into ice water. Let stand in ice water 3 minutes or until cool. Drain well; set aside.

2. In a small bowl combine parsley, rosemary, lime peel and juice, and garlic. Set aside.

3. In a large skillet heat olive oil on medium-high heat. Add beans. Cook for 3 to 4 minutes or until heated through, stirring occasionally. Season with ½ teaspoon each salt and black pepper. Remove from heat. Stir in lime mixture and hazelnuts. Serve with lime wedges.

*Note: To toast nuts, seeds, or coconut, spread them in a single layer on a baking sheet. Bake at 350°F for 5 to 10 minutes, stirring once or twice, until lightly browned. For hazelnuts, remove papery skins by spreading the nuts on a clean towel, then using the towel to rub off the skins.

Per serving: 103 cal., 7 g total fat (1 g sat. fat), 0 mg chol., 299 mg sodium, 10 g carbo., 5 g fiber, 3 g pro.

Walnut-Sage Potatoes

Nutty, fruity, earthy, and mushroomy are the adjectives used most often to describe the incredible flavor of Gruyère cheese.

Prep: 25 minutes **Bake:** 1 hour 10 minutes
Stand: 10 minutes **Oven:** 350°F
Makes: 8 to 10 servings

- 2 **pounds potatoes (6 medium)**
- 3 **tablespoons walnut oil**
- ½ **cup chopped onion (1 medium)**
- 2 **cloves garlic, minced**
- 3 **tablespoons all-purpose flour**
- ½ **teaspoon salt**
- ¼ **teaspoon black pepper**
- 2½ **cups milk**
- 3 **tablespoons snipped fresh sage**
- 1 **cup shredded Gruyère cheese (4 ounces)**
- ⅓ **cup broken walnut pieces**
  Fresh sage leaves (optional)

1. If desired, peel potatoes. Thinly slice potatoes (you should have 6 cups). Place slices in a colander. Rinse with cool water; set aside to drain.

2. Preheat oven to 350°F. Grease a 2-quart casserole; set aside. For sauce, in a medium saucepan cook onion and garlic in walnut oil on medium heat until tender but not brown. Stir in flour, salt, and pepper. Add milk all at once. Cook and stir on medium heat until thickened and bubbly. Remove from heat; stir in snipped sage.

3. Layer half of the potatoes in the prepared casserole. Cover with half of the sauce. Sprinkle with half the cheese. Repeat layering with the potatoes and sauce. Reserve remaining cheese.

4. Bake, covered, for 40 minutes. Uncover and bake about 25 minutes more or until potatoes are tender. Sprinkle remaining cheese and nuts. Bake, uncovered, for 5 minutes. Remove from oven; let stand for 10 minutes. If desired, sprinkle with sage leaves.

Per serving: 217 cal., 12 g total fat (3 g sat. fat), 17 mg chol., 187 mg sodium, 20 g carbo., 2 g fiber, 9 g pro.

Walnut-Sage Potatoes

Potato-Goat Cheese Gratin

Chèvre—the French word for "goat"—is the general name for cheeses made from goat's milk.

Prep: 30 minutes Cook: 20 minutes
Bake: 1 hour 25 minutes Stand: 20 minutes
Oven: 400°F Makes: 8 servings

- 3 large leeks (white part only), trimmed, halved lengthwise, and thinly sliced (1¼ cups)
- 1 tablespoon all-purpose flour
- 1½ cups fat-free milk
- ½ teaspoon salt
- ¼ black pepper
- ⅛ teaspoon ground nutmeg
- 1 clove garlic, minced
- 2¼ pounds Yukon gold potatoes, peeled and cut in ⅛-inch slices (4 to 5 medium)
- 1 cup goat cheese (4 ounces)
- ¼ cup panko or soft bread crumbs
- ¼ cup finely shredded Parmesan cheese
  Snipped fresh parsley

1. Preheat oven to 400°F. In a nonstick skillet cook leeks in 1 tablespoon olive oil on medium-low heat 20 minutes, or until tender and beginning to brown, stirring occasionally. Remove from heat.

2. Place flour in a bowl. Whisk 2 tablespoons of the milk into the flour. Whisk in remaining milk, salt, pepper, nutmeg, and garlic.

3. Coat a 2-quart casserole or gratin dish with nonstick cooking spray. Arrange half the potato slices in dish. Sprinkle with leeks and goat cheese. Pour half the milk mixture over potatoes, leeks, and cheese. Layer remaining potatoes; pour remaining milk mixture over all. Cover with foil.

4. Bake, covered, for 45 minutes. Remove cover and bake 25 minutes more or until potatoes are tender. In a small bowl stir together bread crumbs and Parmesan cheese. Sprinkle on potatoes. Bake, uncovered, 15 minutes more or until topping is browned. Let stand 10 minutes before serving. Sprinkle with parsley.

Make-ahead directions: Prepare casserole through Step 3. Cover and chill up to 24 hours. Remove from refrigerator and let stand at room temperature for 20 minutes. Preheat oven to 400°F. Bake as instructed in Step 4.

Per serving: 209 cal., 6 g total fat (3 g sat. fat)), 9 mg chol., 278 mg sodium, 32 g carbo., 2 g fiber, 8 g pro.

Roasted Beets and Greens with Spicy Orange Vinaigrette

Once roasted, slip off the beets' skin with your fingers to reveal gloriously deep crimson color.

Prep: 25 minutes **Roast:** 40 minutes
Oven: 400° F **Makes:** 8 servings

1	teaspoon finely shredded orange peel
¼	cup orange juice
3	tablespoons red wine vinegar
4	cloves garlic, minced
1	green onion, finely chopped
1	teaspoon ground cinnamon
½	teaspoon salt
¼	teaspoon cayenne pepper or paprika
½	cup extra virgin olive oil
1½	pounds baby beets, trimmed and roasted* (about 6 medium)
1	head red leaf lettuce or leaf lettuce, torn (8 cups)
3	to 4 small blood oranges and/or oranges, peeled and sliced
½	cup dried cranberries**

1. For Spicy Orange Vinaigrette, in a small bowl combine orange peel, orange juice, vinegar, garlic, green onion, cinnamon, salt, and cayenne pepper. Gradually whisk in olive oil.

2. In a large salad bowl combine beets, lettuce, and orange slices. Toss with some of the Spicy Orange Vinaigrette; pass remaining vinaigrette. Sprinkle with dried cranberries.

*Roasted Beets: Preheat oven to 400°F. Scrub beets but do not remove the skins; cut in halves or wedges. Place in 3-quart rectangular baking dish. Drizzle beets with 3 tablespoons olive oil. Sprinkle with ¼ teaspoon each salt and black pepper. Toss lightly to coat. Cover dish with foil. Bake 40 to 45 minutes or until tender. Cool, and peel before assembling salad.

**Note: If desired, pour boiling water over dried cranberries and let stand 5 minutes. Drain.

Per serving: 180 cal., 14 g total fat (2 g sat. fat), 0 mg chol., 153 mg sodium, 14 g carbo., 3 g fiber, 2 g pro.

Roasted Beets and Greens with
Spicy Orange Vinaigrette

Spinach Salad with Brie Toast

The combination of warm, gooey cheese plus crisp, crunchy toast and cool, tender greens makes this salad a true adventure in textures.

Prep: 30 minutes **Broil:** 1 minute
Makes: 8 servings

⅔	cup fresh or frozen cranberries
¼	cup sugar
¼	cup white wine vinegar
¼	cup orange juice
2	teaspoons Dijon mustard
¾	cup canola or olive oil
2	teaspoons finely snipped fresh sage
½	teaspoon kosher salt or salt
¼	teaspoon freshly ground black pepper
16	¼-inch slices baguette, toasted
8	ounces Brie cheese, cut into 16 wedges
10	cups baby spinach
½	cup dried cranberries
¼	cup shelled pumpkin seeds (pepitas), toasted* (optional)

1. For the dressing, in a saucepan combine cranberries, sugar, and vinegar. Cook and stir on medium heat for 5 minutes or until cranberries soften and begin to pop. Remove from heat; cool.

2. Transfer cranberry mixture to blender. Blend on high until nearly smooth. Add juice and mustard; process to blend. With blender running, slowly pour in oil until slightly thickened and creamy. Transfer to bowl. Whisk in sage, salt, and pepper.

3. Place toasted bread slices on a baking sheet; top with cheese. Broil 5 to 6 inches from the heat for 1 to 2 minutes or until cheese is slightly melted.

4. Toss spinach, dried cranberries, and, if desired, pumpkin seeds with ¾ cup of the dressing. Serve with toast. Pass additional dressing.

***Note:** To toast pumpkin seeds, preheat oven to 350°F. Spread pumpkin seeds in a single layer on a baking sheet. Bake for 7 to 8 minutes or until lightly browned, stirring once.

Per serving (with 2 Brie toasts): 264 cal., 18 g total fat (6 g sat. fat), 28 mg chol., 357 mg sodium, 19 g carbo., 2 g fiber, 8 g pro.

Spinach Salad with Brie Toast

Butterhead Salad with Smoky Ranch Dressing

Creamy, cool, fresh, and slightly smoky—what's not to love about this salad? It is sure to become a family favorite, and one they'll ask for often.

Start to Finish: 20 minutes **Makes:** 8 servings

- 1 **clove garlic, peeled**
- ½ **teaspoon salt**
- 1 **cup buttermilk**
- ⅓ **cup mayonnaise**
- ⅓ **cup sour cream**
- 2 **tablespoons snipped fresh parsley**
- 2 **tablespoons snipped fresh chives**
- 2 **tablespoons green onion, thinly sliced (1)**
- 1 **teaspoon white wine vinegar**
- ½ **teaspoon smoked paprika**
- ¼ **teaspoon black pepper**
- 4 **heads butterhead (Boston or Bibb) lettuce, torn (about 24 cups)**
- 1 **cup yellow pear tomatoes, halved**

1. For Smoky Ranch Dressing, place garlic clove on a cutting board and use the side of a wide knife to smash. Sprinkle the ½ teaspoon salt on garlic.

Use side of knife to mash and rub into a paste. Transfer to a medium bowl. Add buttermilk, mayonnaise, sour cream, parsley, chives, green onion, vinegar, paprika, and pepper to garlic paste. Whisk until well combined.

2. Toss lettuce with tomatoes. Serve with Smoky Ranch Dressing.

Note: Dressing may be made up to 1 week in advance. Store in an airtight container in the refrigerator.

Per serving: 70 cal., 5 g total fat (1 g sat. fat), 5 mg chol., 158 mg sodium, 4 g carbo., 1 g fiber, 2 g pro.

Sicilian Escarole Salad

Sicilian Escarole Salad

Escarole—a member of the endive family—adds an enticing, peppery punch to this hearty main-dish salad.

Prep: 20 minutes **Makes:** 12 to 16 servings

1 recipe Dressing
6 cups torn escarole
6 cups torn leaf lettuce
1 English cucumber or cucumber, quartered lengthwise and sliced into ½-inch chunks
1 cup pitted ripe olives or oil-cured black olives, chopped
1 cup thinly sliced red or thinly sliced Vidalia onion
3 cups assorted stir-ins: such as chopped roasted red sweet peppers, drained and rinsed cannellini beans, drained and flaked oil-packed Italian tuna, Parmesan croutons, tomato slices, snipped fresh basil, snipped fresh oregano, chopped salami, chopped mortadella, cubed Asiago cheese, and shredded provolone cheese

1. Prepare Dressing. In a very large salad bowl combine escarole, lettuce, cucumber, olives, and onion. Add desired stir-ins. Just before serving, pour Dressing over salad and toss well.

Dressing: In a screw-top jar combine ⅓ cup olive oil; 2 tablespoons white wine vinegar; one 2-ounce can anchovy fillets, drained and chopped; 3 cloves garlic, minced; ½ teaspoon each dried basil and oregano, crushed; ¼ teaspoon sea salt or salt; ¼ teaspoon crushed red pepper; and ⅛ teaspoon black pepper. Cover; shake well.

Per serving (without stir-ins): 93 cal., 8 g total fat (1 g sat. fat)), 4 mg chol., 319 mg sodium, 4 g carbo., 2 g fiber, 2 g pro.

Fresh Citrus and Cranberry Salad

When peeling fresh ginger for grating, gently remove the thin beige skin with the tip of a spoon. Ginger's most intense flavor lies just beneath the skin, and using a paring knife cuts too much of it away.

Prep: 25 minutes **Chill:** 1 hour **Makes:** 8 servings

- 2 cups fresh or frozen cranberries, thawed
- 4 oranges
- 1 cup thinly sliced celery (2 stalks)
- ⅓ cup finely chopped red onion
- ¼ cup sugar
- 2 tablepoons fresh lemon juice
- 1 teaspoon grated fresh ginger
- 1 5-ounce package baby arugula
- ¼ cup fresh mint leaves, chopped
- 2 tablespoons walnut oil or olive oil

1. For cranberry topping, place cranberries in a food processor and process until coarsely chopped. Transfer cranberries to a medium bowl.

2. Remove the peel from oranges. Section oranges over bowl to catch juice. Add orange sections and juice to cranberries. Stir in celery, onion, sugar, lemon juice, and ginger. Cover bowl and refrigerate at least 1 hour or up to 2 days.

3. Place arugula and mint in a large bowl. Add oil and toss to coat. Top with cranberry mixture.

Per serving: 92 cal., 4 g total fat (0 g sat. fat)), 0 mg chol., 16 mg sodium, 15 g carbo., 3 g fiber, 1 g pro.

Savory Plum Salad

The slightly bitter flavor of radicchio [rah-DEE-kee-oh] is at its best when the deep purple chicory is purchased in midwinter to early spring.

Start to Finish: 25 minutes **Makes:** 6 to 8 servings

- 1 large or 2 medium heads radicchio (about 4 cups)
- ½ a 6-ounce package baby spinach (4 cups)
- 4 plums, quartered and pitted
- ½ cup pecan halves, toasted
- 6 slices bacon, crisp-cooked and crumbled
- 2 tablespoons raspberry vinegar
- 1 tablespoon Dijon mustard
- ½ teaspoon salt
- ¼ teaspoon black pepper
- ⅓ cup extra virgin olive oil
- ¼ cup crumbled Gorgonzola cheese

1. Cut radicchio in wedges. Place in a salad bowl with spinach, plums, pecans, and bacon.

2. In a small bowl whisk together vinegar, mustard, salt, and pepper. Whisk in olive oil; drizzle on salad. Toss gently to combine. Sprinkle cheese.

Per serving: 265 cal., 24 g total fat (4 g sat. fat)), 13 mg chol., 531 mg sodium, 9 g carbo., 2 g fiber, 6 g pro.

Savory Plum Salad

Fennel Slaw

When crisp, sweet fennel meets firm, salty olives, a perfectly balanced culinary marriage is made.

Prep: 25 minutes **Chill:** 1 hour
Makes: 5½ cups or 8 servings

    2   medium fennel bulbs (about 1 pound each)
    1   cup large green olives, pitted and sliced
    ⅓   cup chopped fresh parsley
    ⅓   cup olive oil
    3   tablespoons red wine vinegar
    4   cloves garlic, minced
    ¼   teaspoon salt
    ¼   teaspoon crushed red pepper

1. Trim any brown spots from fennel and cut a thin slice off bases of bulbs. Discard green stems. Cut fennel bulbs in half lengthwise, then cut crosswise into thin slices. (You should have about 3 cups.)

2. Combine fennel, olives, and parsley in a large bowl. In a small bowl whisk together oil, vinegar, garlic, salt, and crushed red pepper. Add to fennel mixture; toss to coat. Cover and refrigerate 1 to 24 hours.

Per serving: 128 cal., 12 g total fat (2 g sat. fat)), 0 mg chol., 391 mg sodium, 6 g carbo., 3 g fiber, 1 g pro.

Port Baked Pears or Apples

Sweet and spicy Seckel pears possess a firm texture that makes them a perfect choice for baking.

Prep: 15 minutes **Cook:** 50 minutes
Makes: 6 servings

    2   cups port wine or apple juice
    1   teaspoon apricot preserves (if using
        apple juice)
    6   tiny Seckel pears or small pears
        (about 12 ounces)
    6   ounces Gorgonzola or cheddar cheese,
        cut into small wedges
    6   walnut halves

1. In a saucepan bring port to boiling. Reduce heat and simmer, at a low boil, for about 50 minutes or until liquid is reduced to ¼ cup. If using apple juice, stir in apricot preserves.

2. To serve, if desired, core pears from bottom, leaving top and stems intact. Place pears in 6 small rimmed dishes. Drizzle about 2 teaspoons of the reduced mixture over the pears. Serve with a small wedge of cheese and a walnut half.

Per serving: 270 cal., 10 g total fat (5 g sat. fat)), 21 mg chol., 399 mg sodium, 20 g carbo., 1 g fiber, 7 g pro.

Baked Apples with Feta and Thyme

Because it is cured and stored in brine, feta is sometimes called "pickled cheese."

Prep: 20 minutes **Bake:** 30 minutes
Cook: 10 minutes **Oven:** 350°F **Makes:** 6 servings

    3   small to medium cooking apples
    2   teaspoons snipped fresh thyme
    1   cup apple cider or apple juice
    ⅓   cup raisins and/or dried cherries
    ½   cup feta cheese, crumbled (2 ounces)
    2   teaspoons olive oil
        Apple cider or apple juice

1. Preheat oven to 350°F. Cut apples in half lengthwise and cut out the cores to make a deep well in each.* Sprinkle cut sides of apples with 1 teaspoon of the thyme. Place apple halves, cut sides down, in a 2-quart rectangular baking dish. Pour apple cider over apples in baking dish. Bake, covered, 25 minutes. Remove from oven and turn apples cut sides up. Spoon apple cider in bottom of dish over apples.

2. Meanwhile, in a small bowl combine raisins and/or cherries, cheese, and remaining thyme. Toss mixture with olive oil. Spoon mixture into centers of apple halves, mounding as needed. Bake apples, uncovered, about 5 minutes more or just until the filling is heated through.

3. Transfer apple halves to serving platter. If desired, strain juices through a strainer lined with 100%-cotton cheesecloth. Measure juices. If necessary, add enough apple cider to make ¾ cup. Bring to boiling in a small saucepan on high heat. Continue boiling about 10 minutes or until mixture measures ¼ cup and slightly thickens. Spoon over apple halves to serve.

*Note: Use a melon baller to make a deep well in each apple half.

Per serving: 111 cal., 4 g total fat (2 g sat. fat)), 8 mg chol., 107 mg sodium, 19 g carbo., 2 g fiber, 2 g pro.

Potato-Fennel Soup

This rich and filling soup—its texture like velvet— makes a satisfying starter to light holiday meals.

Prep: 15 minutes **Roast:** 1 hour **Cook:** 25 minutes
Makes: 6 servings **Oven:** 400°F

Potato-Fennel Soup

- 1 medium beet, trimmed (about 8 ounces)
- 2 medium heads garlic (16 cloves)
- 3 cups peeled and diced potatoes (about 1 pound)
- 1 medium fennel bulb, sliced (discard leafy top) (1½ cups)
- 4 14-ounce cans reduced-sodium chicken broth
- ⅓ cup whipping cream
   Salt
   Black pepper
- 1 tablespoon snipped fresh chives (optional)

1. Preheat oven to 400°F. Wrap beet loosely in foil. Roast for 1 hour or until tender; cool. Peel and cut into bite-size strips; set aside.

2. Separate garlic heads into cloves; peel cloves. In a large saucepan combine garlic, potatoes, fennel, and broth. Bring to boiling; reduce heat. Cover and simmer for 20 to 25 minutes or until vegetables are very tender. Cool slightly.

3. Transfer one-third of the mixture to a blender or food processor. Cover and blend or process until smooth. Repeat with remaining mixture. Return blended mixture to saucepan. Stir in cream. Season to taste with salt and pepper. Heat through. Ladle soup into bowls. Sprinkle with beet strips and, if desired, snipped chives.

Per serving: 163 cal., 7 g total fat (4 g sat. fat)), 18 mg chol., 1,172 mg sodium, 21 g carbo., 2 g fiber, 5 g pro.

Italian Spinach Soup

Italian Spinach Soup

Beauty, grace, and sophistication dressed in a cloak of healthfulness—this exquisite soup has it all.

Start to Finish: 35 minutes
Makes: 5½ cups or 6 servings

½	cup chopped onion (1 medium)
4	cloves garlic, minced
2	teaspoons dried Italian seasoning, crushed
2	tablespoons butter
2	tablespoons dry sherry (optional)
2	14-ounce cans chicken broth
1	large potato, peeled and chopped
2	9-ounce packages fresh spinach or 1¼ pounds fresh spinach, washed and trimmed
2	cups watercress, tough stems removed
2	ounces Parmesan cheese, shaved
2	small tomatoes, quartered, seeded, and thinly sliced

1. In a 4-quart Dutch oven cook onion, garlic, and Italian seasoning in hot butter on medium heat 5 minutes or until onion is tender, stirring occasionally.

2. If using sherry, remove Dutch oven from heat; slowly pour in sherry. Return to heat; cook and stir 1 minute. Add broth and potato. Bring to boiling. Simmer, covered, 10 minutes or until potato is tender. Remove from heat.

3. Set aside 2 cups of the spinach. Stir remaining spinach, half at a time, into soup until wilted. Cook about 5 minutes.

4. Transfer soup, half at a time, to food processor or blender; cover and process or blend until smooth. Return to Dutch oven; heat through. Season with salt.

5. To serve, top with reserved spinach, watercress, Parmesan cheese, and tomatoes.

Per serving: 151 cal., 7 g total fat (4 g sat. fat)), 18 mg chol., 881 mg sodium, 16 g carbo., 4 g fiber, 8 g pro.

Beet and Apple Soup with Horseradish Cream

Adorned in the colors of Christmas, this silky-smooth pureed soup sets the stage for an incredible feast.

Start to Finish: 50 minutes
Makes: 9 cups or 8 servings

2½	pounds beets (10 medium)
½	cup chopped sweet onion (1 medium)
1	medium potato, peeled and chopped
1	cup cooking apple, such as Granny Smith or Gala, peeled, cored, and chopped (1 small)
3	14-ounce cans reduced-sodium chicken broth
2	tablespoons dry sherry or white balsamic vinegar
	Salt
	Black pepper
1	8-ounce carton sour cream
2	tablespoons prepared horseradish
¼	teaspoon cayenne pepper
1	recipe Skillet Beets (optional)

1. Peel eight of the beets and cut each in 1-inch pieces. (Reserve remaining two beets for Skillet Beets, if using). In a 4-quart Dutch oven combine the chopped beets, onion, potato, apple, and broth; bring to boiling. Reduce heat. Simmer, covered, 25 to 30 minutes or until tender. Cool 5 minutes.

2. Transfer soup, half at a time, to food processor. Cover; process until smooth. Return to Dutch oven. Stir in sherry. Season to taste with salt and black pepper. Heat through.

3. For Horseradish Cream, in small a bowl combine sour cream, horseradish, and cayenne pepper; stir about ½ cup cream mixture into hot soup. Set remaining cream mixture aside.

4. To serve, top soup with horseradish cream and Skillet Beets.

Per serving: 222 cal., 9 g total fat (5 g sat. fat)), 17 mg chol., 729 mg sodium, 31 g carbo., 6 g fiber, 7 g pro.

Skillet Beets: Trim tops from two reserved beets to leave 1 inch of stem. Peel and thinly slice beets lengthwise from top to bottom. In a skillet cook beet slices in 2 tablespoons hot oil on medium heat 8 minutes or until tender, turning once.

glorious appetizers and drinks

Savory bites—little morsels loaded with big flavors—are the perfect solution to holiday entertaining. Whether hot or cold, individual or shared, they have what it takes to please. Dish them up for sumptuous snacks, light meals, or beautiful buffet stars. Add a sensational sipper and let the party begin.

2. Bake for 15 minutes, stirring twice. Spread nuts on a large piece of foil to cool. Store in an airtight container at room temperature for up to 2 weeks or freeze up to 3 months.

Per ¼ cup: 223 cal., 20 g total fat (4 g sat. fat), 5 mg chol., 104 mg sodium, 9 g carbo., 3 g fiber, 6 g pro.

Dilled Onion Cheese Ball

The iconic cheese ball—party staple of the '60s—is again the belle of the ball. Rich and fruity Gouda cheese makes this one especially scrumptious.

Prep: 35 minutes **Chill:** 4 hours **Stand:** 15 minutes
Makes: about 30 (1-tablespoon) servings

  1 **8-ounce package cream cheese**
  1 **cup Gouda cheese, finely shredded
     (4 ounces)**
  ¼ **cup butter**
  1 **tablespoon milk**
  ½ **teaspoon Worcestershire sauce for chicken**
  2 **tablespoons thinly sliced green onion (1)**
  2 **tablespoons snipped fresh dill or
     2 teaspoons dried dillweed**
  ½ **cup chopped toasted almonds
     Assorted crackers and/or flatbread**

1. In a large mixing bowl let cream cheese, shredded cheese, and butter stand at room temperature for 30 minutes. Add milk and Worcestershire sauce. Beat with an electric mixer on medium until light and fluffy. Stir in green onion and dill. Cover and chill for 4 to 24 hours.

2. Before serving, shape cheese mixture into a ball. Roll ball in nuts and let stand 15 minutes. Serve with crackers or flatbread.

Make-ahead directions: Prepare as directed in Step 1. Wrap cheese ball in plastic wrap. Freeze for up to 1 month. To serve, thaw the cheese ball in the refrigerator overnight. Unwrap and roll in nuts. Let the cheese stand for 15 minutes at room temperature before serving.

Per tablespoon spread: 63 cal., 6 g total fat (3 g sat. fat), 16 mg chol., 2 mg sodium, 1 g carbo., 0 g fiber, 2 g pro.

Chili Mixed Nuts

Chili Mixed Nuts

Some like it hot. Feel free to use hot chili powder if you'd like to turn up the heat on this nutty nosh.

Prep: 10 minutes **Bake:** 15 minutes **Oven:** 325°F
Makes: 3 cups

  2 **tablespoons butter, melted**
  1 **tablespoon chili powder**
  1 **tablespoon lime juice**
  1 **teaspoon garlic salt**
  3 **cups mixed nuts or peanuts**

1. Preheat oven to 325°F. In a small bowl combine melted butter, chili powder, lime juice, and garlic salt. In a 15×10×1-inch baking pan combine butter mixture and nuts. Toss to coat evenly.

Prosciutto-Basil Cheese Ball: Prepare as directed in Step 1, except substitute finely shredded fontina cheese for the Gouda cheese, stir in 2 ounces chopped prosciutto and 2 tablespoons snipped fresh basil along with the green onion, and omit the dill. Substitute chopped toasted pine nuts for the almonds. If desired, serve with apples, crackers, or flatbread.

Caramelized Onion-Blue Cheese Dip

Often, dried herbs will suffice, but this creamy concoction will be extra-delectable if you use fresh thyme or sage. Go ahead and spurge!

Prep: 15 minutes **Cook:** 18 minutes
Makes: 2 cups

- 1 tablespoon olive oil
- 1 large sweet onion, halved and cut into thin slivers
- 8 ounces cremini mushrooms, chopped
- ½ of an 8-ounce package reduced-fat cream cheese (Neufchâtel), softened
- ⅓ cup crumbled blue cheese
- ¼ cup fat-free milk
- 1 teaspoon snipped fresh thyme or sage
- ⅛ teaspoon salt
- ⅛ teaspoon freshly ground black pepper
  Pear slices, melba toast, and/or whole grain crackers

1. In a large nonstick skillet heat olive oil on medium heat. Add onion. Cover and cook in hot oil for 10 minutes, stirring occasionally. Uncover and add mushrooms. Cook, uncovered, for 8 to 10 minutes or until mushrooms are tender and onion is golden brown, stirring occasionally.

2. Add cream cheese, blue cheese, milk, thyme, salt, and pepper to onion mixture. Cook and stir over low heat until mixture melts. Serve warm with pear slices, melba toast, and/or whole grain crackers.

Per ¼ cup: 99 cal., 7 g total fat (3 g sat. fat), 15 mg chol., 172 mg sodium, 6 g carbo., 1 g fiber, 4 g pro.

Caramelized Onion-Blue Cheese Dip

Cranberry-Pistachio Pâté

Country-style pâté—such as this sumptuous selection—may be made up to three days ahead, and chilled while its flavor intensifies in the fridge.

Prep: 30 minutes **Bake:** 1½ hours
Chill: 12 hours **Oven:** 350°F
Makes: 24 servings

    Nonstick cooking spray
1 egg, lightly beaten
¾ cup dried cranberries
½ cup chopped shallot or onion
½ cup chopped pistachio nuts
⅓ cup port wine or cranberry juice
¼ cup half-and-half or light cream
¼ cup fine dry bread crumbs
2 teaspoons dried sage leaves, crushed, or
   ½ teaspoon ground sage
1 teaspoon salt
1 teaspoon coarsely ground black pepper
2 cloves garlic, minced

1 pound lean ground beef
1 pound lean ground pork
   Stone-ground mustard

1. Preheat oven to 350°F. Lightly coat a 9×5×3-inch loaf pan with cooking spray; set aside.

2. In a large bowl combine egg, cranberries, shallot, nuts, wine, half-and-half, bread crumbs, sage, salt, pepper, and garlic; mix well. Add ground beef and pork. Mix well. Press mixture into prepared pan. Cover tightly with foil.

3. Bake for 1½ hours. Remove pan from oven; cool slightly. Uncover; carefully pour off drippings, leaving pâté in pan. Cover pâté loosely with foil. To serve as a weight, place several heavy cans of food in another 9×5×3-inch loaf pan. Place on top of the covered pâté. Chill for 12 to 24 hours.

4. Remove weighted pan and foil. If necessary, loosen sides of pâté. Invert onto a serving platter. Cut in half lengthwise, then into thin slices. Serve pâté with stone-ground mustard.

Per serving: 135 cal., 9 g total fat (3 g sat. fat), 36 mg chol., 155 mg sodium, 6 g carbo., 1 g fiber, 8 g pro.

Cranberry-Pistachio Pâté

Bruschetta

This universally loved Italian specialty will tastefully stretch your entertaining budget.

Prep: 25 minutes **Bake:** 7 minutes **Oven:** 425°F
Makes: 8 to 10 servings

1 8-ounce loaf baguette-style French bread
2 tablespoons olive oil
   Freshly ground black pepper
   Toppings, such as Shrimp, Basil Pesto and White Beans, Fresh Tomato and Olives, or Dried Fig and Pistachio
   Small fresh basil leaves (optional)

1. Preheat oven to 425°F. For crostini, bias-slice the bread into ½-inch-thick slices. Arrange in a single layer on an ungreased baking sheet. Lightly brush one side of each bread slice with the olive oil. Lightly sprinkle oiled side with pepper. Bake, uncovered, for 4 minutes. Turn slices over and

Bruschetta

bake for 3 to 4 minutes more or until crisp and light brown.

2. Prepare one or more of the toppings. Spoon onto toasted bread just before serving.

Shrimp: In a medium bowl stir together 8 ounces large peeled and deveined cooked shrimp, chopped; 1 tablespoon olive oil; 2 teaspoons white wine vinegar; ¼ teaspoon salt; and ¼ teaspoon black pepper. Set aside. Halve 2 large cloves of garlic and rub toasts with cut sides before topping with shrimp mixture.

Per serving: 282 cal., 18 g total fat (4 g sat. fat), 36 mg chol., 503 mg sodium, 24 g carbo., 3 g fiber, 9 g pro.

Basil Pesto and White Beans: In a small bowl stir together a 9-ounce container (1 cup) basil pesto; 1 finely chopped hard-cooked egg; and 1 teaspoon lemon juice, sherry vinegar, or red wine vinegar. In another small bowl stir together half of a 19-ounce can cannellini (white kidney) beans or half of a 15-ounce can great Northern beans, rinsed and drained (1 cup), 1 tablespoon thinly sliced green onion or chopped shallot, 1 tablespoon olive oil, and ⅛ teaspoon crushed red pepper.

Fresh Tomato and Olives: In a small bowl stir together 1 cup seeded and finely chopped tomatoes (2 medium); 1 cup coarsely chopped assorted pitted ripe olives (such as kalamata, Greek, or Mission); ⅓ cup finely chopped red onion; 2 tablespoons snipped fresh cilantro or parsley; 2 tablespoons balsamic vinegar or red wine vinegar; and 2 cloves garlic, minced.

Dried Fig and Pistachio: In a medium bowl place 3 ounces cream cheese, 2 ounces fontina or provolone cheese, and 3 ounces goat cheese (chèvre); let stand at room temperature for 30 minutes. In a small bowl stir together ¼ cup snipped figs and 1 tablespoon balsamic vinegar; let stand at room temperature for 30 minutes. Beat with an electric mixer on low speed until well combined; stir in figs. Serve with ¼ cup chopped pistachio nuts.

Double-Quick Shrimp Cocktail

1. In a small bowl stir together sour cream, horseradish, snipped chives, and lemon juice. Place the sauces in a 4-cup shallow serving bowl.* If desired, cover and chill up to 4 hours before serving.

2. To serve, place bowl containing dip mixture on a platter. Arrange shrimp around bowl. Garnish with chives and/or lemon wedges.

Note: It's easier than it looks to present two sauces in the same bowl. Tilt the bowl slightly and put the cocktail sauce in one side. Then tilt the bowl the opposite way and add the sour cream sauce.

Per serving: 37 cal., 1 g total fat (1 g sat. fat), 36 mg chol., 119 mg sodium, 2 g carbo., 0 g fiber, 4 g pro.

Asian Chicken Wings

Five-spice powder—a pungent blend of cinnamon, cloves, fennel seeds, star anise, and Szechwan peppercorns—is theingredxient thatr leads to this recipe's success.

Prep: 25 minutes **Cook:** 20 minutes
Makes: 12 servings

- 12 chicken wings (about 2 pounds)
- 1½ cups water
- ⅔ cup soy sauce
- 4 slices fresh ginger
- 1 leek, cut up
- 1 tablespoon sugar
- 1 tablespoon vinegar
- 2 or 3 dried red chiles
- ½ teaspoon purchased five-spice powder
- 2 cloves garlic, minced
  Bottled teriyaki sauce (optional)

1. Cut off and discard tips of chicken wings. Cut wings at joints, if desired, to form 24 pieces.

2. For sauce, in a 4-quart Dutch oven combine water, soy sauce, ginger, leek, sugar, vinegar, chiles, five-spice powder, and garlic. Bring to boiling. Add chicken. Return to boiling; reduce heat. Simmer, covered, 20 to 25 minutes or until chicken is no longer pink.

Double-Quick Shrimp Cocktail

Two-tone dip? Your guest will adore this clever rendition of the classic party favorite.

Start to Finish: 15 minutes
Makes: about 30 servings

- 1 8-ounce carton sour cream
- ¼ cup prepared horseradish
- 2 tablespoons snipped chives or thinly sliced green onion tops
- 1 tablespoon lemon juice
- 1 12-ounce jar seafood cocktail sauce or chili sauce
- 1½ pounds (60 to 75) frozen peeled and cooked shrimp with tails, thawed
  Chives and/or lemon wedges

3. Using a slotted spoon, remove chicken wings from the Dutch oven. Place wings in a container. If desired, serve wings with bottled teriyaki sauce for dipping.

Per serving: 123 cal., 9 g total fat (2 g sat. fat), 58 mg chol., 204 mg sodium, 0 g carbo., 0 g fiber, 10 g pro.

Apricot-Glazed Ham Balls

Grind ham by pulsing it in a food processor or chop the ham with a knife until it is the texture of ground beef.

Prep: 20 minutes **Bake:** 20 minutes
Oven: 425°F
Cook: 4 to 5 hours (low) or 1½ to 2 hours (high)
Makes: 30 meatballs

- 1   **egg, beaten**
- ½   **cup graham cracker crumbs**
- 2   **tablespoons unsweetened pineapple juice**
- 1   **teaspoon dry mustard**
- ¼   **teaspoon salt**
- ½   **pound ground fully cooked ham**
- ½   **pound ground pork**
- ½   **cup snipped dried apricots**
- 1   **18-ounce jar apricot preserves**
- ⅓   **cup unsweetened pineapple juice**
- 1   **tablespoon cider vinegar**
- ½   **teaspoon ground ginger**

1. Preheat oven to 350°F. For meatballs, in a bowl combine egg, graham cracker crumbs, the 2 tablespoons pineapple juice, dry mustard, and salt. Add ground ham, ground pork, and snipped apricots; mix well. Shape into 30 meatballs.* Arrange meatballs in a single layer on a 15×10×1-inch baking pan. Bake, uncovered, for 20 minutes. Drain well. Place meatballs a 3½- or 4-quart slow cooker.

2. For sauce, in a small bowl combine apricot preserves, the ⅓ cup pineapple juice, vinegar, and ginger. Pour sauce over meatballs.

3. Cover and cook on low-heat setting for 4 to 5 hours or on high-heat setting for 1½ to 2 hours.

4. Serve immediately or keep covered on low-heat setting up to 2 hours. Stir just before serving. Serve with wooden food picks.

*Note: For uniformly shaped meatballs, shape the meat mixture into a 6×5-inch rectangle on a piece of waxed paper. Cut the meat into 1-inch cubes, then use your hands to roll each cube into a ball.

Per meatball: 86 cal., 2 g total fat (1 g sat. fat), 15 mg chol., 151 mg sodium, 15 g carbo., 0 g fiber, 3 g pro.

Apricot-Glazed Ham Balls

Ginger-Glazed Cocktail Ribs

Ginger-Glazed Cocktail Ribs

Jarred preserves caramelize on these juicy riblets to form a magnificent mahogany-color glaze. Make it easy by asking your butcher to cut the ribs for you.

Prep: 20 minutes **Bake:** 1¼ hours **Oven:** 350°F
Makes: about 30 servings

2½ to 3 pounds meaty pork loin back ribs
    or spareribs
    Salt
    Ground black pepper
¼ cup finely chopped onion
1 clove garlic, minced
2 teaspoons olive oil or cooking oil
⅓ cup bottled chili sauce
⅓ cup apricot or peach preserves
1 tablespoon soy sauce
1 teaspoon grated fresh ginger or
¼ teaspoon ground ginger

1. Preheat oven to 350°F. Cut ribs into single-rib portions. Sprinkle ribs with salt and pepper. Arrange ribs, meaty sides up, in a shallow roasting pan. Roast about 1 hour or until tender.

2. Meanwhile, for glaze, in a small saucepan cook and stir onion and garlic in hot oil on medium heat about 3 minutes or until onion is tender. Stir in chili sauce, preserves, soy sauce, and ginger. Cook until glaze is bubbly.

3. Brush ribs generously with glaze. Bake ribs for 15 minutes more, brushing once or twice with glaze during baking time.

Make-ahead directions: Prepare the ribs as directed through Step 3. Cool and place in an airtight container; cover. Chill for up to 3 days. To serve, preheat oven to 350°F. Place ribs in a large baking pan and bake about 5 minutes or until heated through.

Per serving: 54 cal., 2 g total fat (1 g sat. fat), 11 mg chol., 95 mg sodium, 3 g carbo., 0 g fiber, 5 g pro.

Maryland Crab Cakes

The key to making incredible crab cakes is gentle mixing. Handle the mixture as little—and as quickly—as you can.

Prep: 30 minutes **Cook:** 6 minutes per batch
Makes: 12 servings

- 1 egg, lightly beaten
- 2 tablespoons mayonnaise
- 1 tablespoon snipped fresh parsley
- 2 teaspoons seafood seasoning
- 1½ teaspoons snipped fresh thyme
- 2 slices soft white bread
- 1 pound cooked lump crabmeat or 3 (6-ounce) cans crabmeat, drained and cartilage removed
- 1 tablespoon peanut oil or cooking oil
  Bottled tartar sauce (optional)

1. In a large bowl combine egg, mayonnaise, parsley, seafood seasoning, and thyme. Remove and discard crusts from bread. Tear bread into very small pieces; stir into egg mixture. Add crabmeat; gently mix with your hands, keeping crab pieces whole. Shape crab mixture into twelve ½-inch-thick cakes.

2. In a large nonstick skillet heat oil on medium heat. Add half of the crab cakes; cook about 6 minutes or until golden brown and heated through, turning once. If cakes brown too quickly, reduce heat to medium-low. Keep warm in a 300°F oven while cooking the remaining crab cakes (add additional oil, if necessary).

3. If desired, serve crab cakes with tartar sauce.

Per serving: 82 cal., 4 g total fat (1 g sat. fat), 56 mg chol., 263 mg sodium, 2 g carbo., 0 g fiber, 9 g pro.

Sweet and Sassy Meatballs

Pleasing people does not get any easier than this. Be prepared for these roly-poly orbs to disappear fast. If you're serving big eaters, consider making a double batch.

Start to Finish: 30 minutes **Makes:** 64 meatballs

- 1 16-ounce bottle jellied cranberry sauce
- 1 18-ounce bottle barbecue sauce
- 2 1-pound packages frozen cooked meatballs, thawed (32 per pound)

1. For sauce, in a large skillet stir together cranberry sauce and barbecue sauce. Cook on medium heat until cranberry sauce is melted, stirring occasionally.

2. Add meatballs to sauce. Cook, uncovered, about 10 minutes or until meatballs are heated through, stirring occasionally. Serve immediately or keep meatballs warm in a slow cooker to serve.

Make-ahead directions: Prepare as directed in Step 1. Stir in frozen or thawed meatballs. Cover and chill for up to 24 hours. To serve, heat meatballs and sauce in a large skillet on medium heat until heated through, stirring occasionally.

Per 4 meatballs: 60 cal., 4 g total fat (2 g sat. fat), 5 mg chol., 177 mg sodium, 5 g carbo., 1 g fiber, 2 g pro.

Sweet and Sassy Meatballs

Triple-Onion Appetizer Tart

¾ teaspoon salt
½ teaspoon ground nutmeg
½ teaspoon ground black pepper
1 3-ounce package cream cheese, cubed and softened
¾ cup shredded Swiss cheese
¾ cup shredded Monterey Jack cheese with jalapeño
3 eggs, lightly beaten
⅔ cup whipping cream

1. Let refrigerated piecrust stand at room temperature according to package directions. Line a 9-inch pie plate with piecrust; set aside.

2. Preheat oven to 375°F. In a skillet melt butter on medium heat; add onion, leek, shallots, sugar, salt, nutmeg, and pepper. Cook about 8 minutes or until tender but not brown, stirring occasionally. Reduce heat; stir in cream cheese until melted. Stir in Swiss cheese and Monterey Jack cheese until combined. In a bowl combine eggs and whipping cream. Gradually stir in onion mixture until combined. Pour into pastry shell. Fold edge of crust over filling, pleating as necessary.

3. Bake for 40 minutes or until golden brown and a knife inserted near the center comes out clean. Cool on wire rack for 15 minutes; cut into wedges.

Per serving: 203 cal., 16 g total fat (9 g sat. fat), 79 mg chol., 256 mg sodium, 10 g carbo., 0 g fiber, 5 g pro.

Triple-Onion Appetizer Tart

Thanks to ready-made piecrusts, this tantalizing tart is a breeze to prepare. Don't worry about keeping it piping hot—its flavors sing at room temperature too.

Prep: 30 minutes **Bake:** 40 minutes
Cool: 15 minutes **Oven:** 375°F
Makes: 16 appetizer servings

½ of a 15-ounce package rolled refrigerated unbaked piecrusts (1 crust)
¼ cup butter
1 Vidalia onion (or other sweet onion), halved and thinly sliced
1 large leek, halved lengthwise and thinly sliced
2 shallots, thinly sliced
1 teaspoon sugar

Chocolate-Peanut Fondue

Every appetizer buffet benefits from a little bite of something sweet. Preparing this delightful dip is practically effortless.

Start to Finish: 15 minutes **Makes:** 8 servings

8 ounces semisweet chocolate, coarsely chopped
1 14-ounce can sweetened condensed milk
½ cup creamy peanut butter
⅓ cup milk
Assorted dippers (such as cubed pound cake, marshmallows, wafer cookies, cubed brownies, mango pieces, nectarine slices, and/or strawberries)

1. In a heavy medium saucepan melt chocolate on low heat, stirring constantly. Stir in sweetened condensed milk, peanut butter, and milk; heat through. Transfer to fondue pot; keep warm over a fondue burner.

2. Serve immediately with desired dippers. If the fondue mixture thickens, stir in a little additional milk.

Per ¼ cup without dippers: 374 cal., 14 g total fat (8 g sat. fat), 18 mg chol., 84 mg sodium, 60 g carbo., 2 g fiber, 6 g pro.

Chocolate Fondue: Prepare as directed, except omit the peanut butter and ⅓ cup milk.

Chocolate-Liqueur Fondue: Prepare as directed, except omit the peanut butter and stir 2 to 4 tablespoons amaretto, orange, hazelnut, or cherry liqueur into mixture after heating.

S'more Fondue: Prepare as directed, except omit peanut butter. Stir in 1 cup marshmallow creme. Serve with graham crackers or graham stick cookies as dippers.

Olives Wrapped in Cheese Pastry

These salty-rich snacks take a little effort on the front end, but the praise you'll hear on the back end will make it all worthwhile.

Prep: 35 minutes **Bake:** 25 minutes **Oven:** 375°F
Makes: 24 appetizers

1	cup all-purpose flour
1	teaspoon baking powder
3	ounces Gouda cheese, finely shredded (¾ cup)
⅓	cup butter, cut in small pieces
2	tablespoons grated Parmesan cheese
1	tablespoon lemon juice
24	medium pimiento-stuffed green olives
1	egg yolk, beaten

1. Preheat oven to 375°F. Line a baking sheet with parchment paper; set aside. In a food processor combine flour and baking powder. Process briefly to mix. Add Gouda cheese, butter, and Parmesan cheese. Process until combined. With food

processor running add lemon juice, processing until dough forms a ball. Divide dough into 24 equal portions.

2. Drain and rinse olives. Pat olives dry with paper towels. Pat each portion of dough into a 2-inch circle. Place an olive in the center of each circle. Bring dough up around olives; place on prepared baking sheet. Brush wrapped olive with egg yolk. Bake about 25 minutes or until golden brown. Serve warm or at room temperature.

Per appetizer: 64 cal., 4 g total fat (2 g sat. fat), 20 mg chol., 123 mg sodium, 4 g carbo., 0 g fiber, 2 g pro.

Olives Wrapped In Cheese Pastry

Chai Punch

1. In a large saucepan combine water, fennel seeds, cloves, cardamom, 4-inch cinnamon sticks, and ginger. Bring to boiling; reduce heat. Simmer, covered, for 15 minutes.

2. Remove saucepan from heat; add tea leaves. Cover and allow to steep for 30 minutes.

3. Strain tea mixture through a fine-mesh sieve; return to saucepan. Add milk and sugar. Cook and stir on medium heat until sugar is dissolved.

4. Pour into glasses. Garnish glasses with orange peel strips.

Per serving: 82 cal., 1 g total fat (1 g sat. fat), 5 mg chol., 31 mg sodium, 16 g carbo., 0 g fiber, 2 g pro.

Sipping Chocolate

With a cup of this rich and decadent hot chocolate in your hands, you'll feel las if you're drinking dessert.

Start to Finish: 15 minutes
Makes: 8 (about 4-ounce) servings

- 4 **cups half-and-half, light cream, or whole milk**
- 3 **to 4 ounces semisweet chocolate, chopped**
- 3 **to 4 ounces bittersweet chocolate, chopped**
- 1 **tablespoon dark-color corn syrup**
  Grated bittersweet chocolate (optional)

1. In a 2-quart heavy saucepan combine half-and-half, semisweet chocolate, and chopped bittersweet chocolate. Stir in corn syrup. Cook and stir on medium heat until chocolate is melted and mixture is smooth.

2. Serve in warmed mugs. If desired, sprinkle with grated bittersweet chocolate.

Per serving: 270 cal., 23 g total fat (14 g sat. fat), 45 mg chol., 52 mg sodium, 17 g carbo., 3 g fiber, 6 g pro.

Chai Punch

This spicy-sweet Indian tea is perfect to sip while standing around an American Christmas tree.

Prep: 15 minutes **Cook:** 15 minutes
Stand: 30 minutes **Makes:** 8 (8-ounce) servings

- 6 **cups water**
- 2 **teaspoons fennel seeds**
- 12 **whole cloves**
- ½ **teaspoon whole cardamom pods**
- 2 **4-inch cinnamon sticks**
- 2 **2-inch slices fresh ginger**
- ⅓ **cup Darjeeling tea leaves (6 bags)**
- 2 **cups milk**
- ½ **cup raw sugar or granulated sugar**
  Orange peel strips

Hot Cider

If you don't have cheesecloth, place the spices in a round pleated paper coffee filter and tie the top tightly with kitchen string.

Prep: 15 minutes **Cook:** 15 minutes
Makes: 10 (6-ounce) servings

- 8 cups apple cider or apple juice
- 2 tablespoons packed brown sugar
   Peel from 1 lemon, cut into strips
- 6 inches stick cinnamon, broken
- 1 teaspoon whole allspice
- 1 teaspoon whole cloves
- 2 tablespoons butter (optional)
   Cinnamon sticks (optional)

1. In a large saucepan combine apple cider and brown sugar. For spice bag, place lemon peel, stick cinnamon pieces, allspice, and cloves in the center of a double-thick, 6-inch square of 100%-cotton cheesecloth. Tie closed with kitchen string. Add bag to saucepan with cider. Bring to boiling; reduce heat. Simmer, covered, for 15 minutes. Discard spice bag. Serve cider in mugs.

2. If desired, top each serving with about ½ teaspoon of the butter and serve with a cinnamon stick stirrer.

Make-ahead directions: After discarding the spice bag, keep cider warm in a slow cooker on low-heat setting. Or refrigerate the prepared cider for up to 1 week; reheat to serve.

Per serving: 126 cal., 3 g total fat (2 g sat. fat), 6 mg chol., 24 mg sodium, 26 g carbo., 0 g fiber, 0 g pro.

Peppermint-Eggnog Punch

Kids will clamor for this fun and fabulous punch— but make sure you make enough for the grown-ups as well.

Start to Finish: 15 minutes
Makes: 18 (4-ounce) servings

- 1 quart peppermint ice cream
- 1 quart eggnog
- 1 to 2 10-ounce bottles (1¼ to 2½ cups) ginger ale, chilled
   Additional peppermint ice cream (optional)
   Peppermint sticks (optional)

1. In a large chilled bowl place ice cream; stir until softened. Gradually stir in eggnog.

2. Transfer to a punch bowl; add amount of ginger ale to reach desired consistency. If desired, top each serving with additional peppermint ice cream and peppermint sticks.

Per serving: 148 cal., 7 g total fat (5 g sat. fat, 0 g trans fat), 47 mg chol., 63 mg sodium, 17 g carbo., 0 g fiber, 3 g pro.

Peppermint-Eggnog Punch

rise and shine

Christmas morning is a special time to relax and enjoy the company of those you love most. Preserve the day's tranquil mood by making the morning menu as easy and effortless as possible. Each of the wonderful waker-uppers featured here is easy enough to prepare while the rest of the family cleans up from the gift-unwrapping festivities.

Breakfast Pizza, page 51

Southwestern Breakfast Bake

Southwestern Breakfast Bake

Big and bold flavors—like those in this hearty casserole—are always welcome at the breakfast table.

Prep: 20 minutes **Bake:** 45 minutes
Stand: 15 minutes **Oven:** 325°F **Makes:** 8 servings

- 1 **15-ounce can black beans, rinsed and drained**
- ¾ **cup canned enchilada sauce**
- 2 **4-ounce cans diced green chiles**
- ½ **cup thinly sliced green onions (4)**
- 2 **cloves garlic, minced**

- **Several dashes bottled hot pepper sauce (optional)**
- 1 **cup shredded sharp cheddar cheese and/or shredded Monterey Jack cheese with jalapeño peppers (4 ounces)**
- 3 **egg whites**
- 3 **egg yolks**
- 2 **tablespoons all-purpose flour**
- ¼ **teaspoon salt**
- ½ **cup milk**
- 1 **tablespoon snipped fresh cilantro**
- **Sour cream (optional)**
- **Salsa (optional)**
- **Additional snipped fresh cilantro (optional)**

1. Preheat oven to 325°F. In a greased 1½-quart rectangle baking dish combine black beans, enchilada sauce, green chiles, green onions, garlic, and, if desired, hot pepper sauce. Sprinkle with cheese.

2. In a medium mixing bowl beat egg whites with an electric mixer on medium until soft peaks form (tips curl); set aside. In a large mixing bowl combine egg yolks, flour, and salt. Using a wire whisk, beat yolk mixture until combined (mixture will be stiff). Gradually whisk in milk until smooth. Fold egg whites and the 1 tablespoon snipped cilantro into yolk mixture. Carefully pour the egg mixture over the bean mixture in the baking dish.

3. Bake for 45 minutes or until egg mixture appears set when gently shaken. Let stand for 15 minutes before serving. If desired, serve with sour cream, salsa, and additional cilantro.

Per serving: 163 cal., 8 g total fat (4 g sat. fat), 96 mg chol., 488 mg sodium, 15 g carbo., 4 g fiber, 11 g pro.

Breakfast Pizza

If you like, make this pretty pie look even more Christmasy by using half green pepper and half red pepper.

Prep: 25 minutes **Bake:** 18 minutes
Oven: 400°F **Makes:** 6 servings

  4 **ounces plain or peppered bacon, diced**
  ½ **cup chopped green sweet pepper**
  ¼ **cup sliced green onions (2)**
  1 **12-inch prebaked pizza shell**
  1 **8-ounce package cream cheese, softened**
  ¼ **teaspoon Italian herbs**
  1 **egg**
  1 **cup cubed cooked ham**
  1 **cup shredded cheddar cheese (4 ounces)**

1. Preheat oven to 400°F. In a large skillet cook bacon pieces on medium-low heat until crisp. Using a slotted spoon, remove bacon from skillet and drain on paper towels. Drain skillet, reserving about 1 tablespoon drippings. Add sweet pepper and green onions to reserved drippings; cook until tender. Drain and set aside.

2. Place pizza shell on a baking sheet; set aside. In a bowl beat cream cheese with an electric mixer on medium just until smooth. Add Italian herbs and egg, beating until combined. Spread cream cheese mixture on pizza shell. Sprinkle with bacon pieces, sweet pepper, and green onions. Top with ham.

3. Bake for 15 minutes or until cream cheese layer is set. Sprinkle with cheese. Bake 3 minutes more or until cheese melts. Cut into wedges to serve.

Per serving: 410 cal., 27 g total fat (13 g sat. fat), 126 mg chol., 635 mg sodium, 29 g carbo., 1 g fiber, 16 g pro.

Breakfast Pizza

Smoked Salmon Frittata

This elegant egg dish makes a beautiful breakfast—or a quick and easy supper.

Start to Finish: 25 minutes **Makes:** 4 servings

- 6   eggs
- ¼   teaspoon black pepper
     Nonstick cooking spray
- ¼   cup sliced green onions (2)
- 1   4-ounce piece smoked salmon, flaked, with skin and bones removed
- 2   tablespoons snipped fresh dill or 1 teaspoon dried dill
- 1   ounce semi-soft goat cheese (chévre), crumbled

1. In a bowl combine eggs and pepper; set aside.

2. Lightly coat a large broilerproof skillet with cooking spray. Cook onions in skillet on medium heat until tender. Stir in salmon and dill. Pour egg mixture into skillet over salmon. As mixture sets, run a spatula around edge of skillet, lifting egg mixture so the uncooked portion flows underneath. Continue cooking and lifting edges until almost set.

3. Place skillet under the broiler 4 to 5 inches from the heat. Broil for 1 to 2 minutes or just until top is set. Sprinkle with cheese.

Per serving: 166 cal., 10 g total fat (4 g sat. fat), 329 mg chol., 344 mg sodium, 1 g carbo., 0 g fiber, 16 g pro.

Potato-Ham Bake

To trim asparagus, hold the spear's base in one hand and its top in another. Bend the spear—it will snap off exactly where it is supposed to.

Prep: 25 minutes **Bake:** 30 minutes
Stand: 5 minutes **Oven:** 400°F **Makes:** 4 servings

- 1   pound Yukon gold potatoes, sliced
- 1   8-ounce tub light cream cheese spread with chive and onion
- ¾   cup milk
- ¼   cup finely shredded Parmesan cheese
- ¼   teaspoon black pepper
- 1   tablespoon snipped fresh tarragon
- 8   ounces cooked boneless ham, cut into bite-size slices
- 1   pound fresh asparagus spears, trimmed, cut into 2- to 3-inch pieces
     Tarragon sprigs (optional)
     Freshly ground black pepper

1. Preheat oven to 400°F. In a medium saucepan cook potatoes, covered, in a small amount of lightly salted boiling water 5 to 7 minutes, just until tender. Drain; transfer to bowl and set aside.

2. For sauce, in same saucepan combine cream cheese, milk, 2 tablespoons of the Parmesan, and the ¼ teaspoon pepper. Whisk until cheese is melted. Remove from heat; stir in tarragon.

3. Layer potatoes, ham, asparagus, and sauce in a 1½-quart baking dish. Bake, covered, 20 minutes. Uncover; sprinkle remaining Parmesan. Bake 10 to 12 minutes more. Let stand 5 minutes. Top with tarragon and freshly ground black pepper.

Per serving: 346 cal., 16 g total fat (9 g sat. fat), 67 mg chol., 1,162 mg sodium, 30 g carbo., 5 g fiber, 22 g pro.

Potato-Ham Bake

Spicy Sicilian Strata

Spicy Sicilian Strata

To make sure that spinach is drained adequately, press spinach firmly into a fine-mesh sieve until every last drop of liquid is released.

Prep: 35 minutes **Chill:** 2 hours **Bake:** 35 minutes
Stand: 10 minutes **Oven:** 350°F **Makes:** 6 servings

    5   cups cubed French bread (1-inch cubes)
    1   3.5-ounce package sliced pepperoni,
        coarsely chopped
    ¼   cup pepperoncini salad peppers, drained,
        stemmed, and chopped
    ½   a 10-ounce package frozen chopped
        spinach, thawed and well drained
    ¼   cup oil-packed dried tomatoes, drained
        and chopped
    1   cup shredded Italian-blend cheese
        (4 ounces)
    3   eggs, lightly beaten
  1½   cups milk
    1   teaspoon dried Italian seasoning, crushed
    ¼   teaspoon salt
        Dash cayenne pepper
    ¼   cup grated Parmesan cheese

1. Preheat oven to 350°F. Place bread cubes in a 15×10×1-inch baking pan. Bake, uncovered, for 10 minutes, stirring once.

2. Lightly grease a 2-quart square baking dish. Place half of the bread cubes in the dish. Top with half of the pepperoni, half of the pepperoncini, all of the spinach, and all of the tomatoes. Sprinkle with ½ cup of the Italian-blend cheese. Repeat layers with remaining bread, pepperoni, pepperoncini, and Italian-blend cheese.

3. In a large bowl whisk together eggs, milk, Italian seasoning, salt, and cayenne pepper. Slowly pour over layers in dish; lightly press down on top layer using the back of a large spoon. Sprinkle with Parmesan cheese. Cover and chill for 2 to 24 hours.

4. Bake, uncovered, for 35 to 45 minutes or until a knife inserted near the center comes out clean (170°F). Let stand for 10 minutes before serving.

Per serving: 316 cal., 18 g total fat (8 g sat. fat), 146 mg chol., 1,006 mg sodium, 22 g carbo., 2 g fiber, 18 g pro.

Caramel-Pecan French Toast

Caramel rolls are a delightful—but difficult to make—holiday indulgence. This oven-baked breakfast provides all that yummy taste and gooey texture with much less effort.

Prep: 20 minutes **Chill:** 2 hours **Bake:** 30 minutes
Stand: 10 minutes **Oven:** 350°F **Makes:** 8 servings

1	cup packed brown sugar
½	cup butter
2	tablespoons light-color corn syrup
1	cup chopped pecans, toasted
16	½-inch slices French bread
6	eggs, lightly beaten
1½	cups milk
1	teaspoon vanilla
1	tablespoon granulated sugar
1½	teaspoons ground cinnamon
¼	teaspoon ground nutmeg
	Raspberries, maple syrup, and/or toasted chopped pecans (optional)

1. In a medium saucepan combine brown sugar, butter, and corn syrup. Cook and stir until butter is melted and brown sugar is dissolved. Pour into a 3-quart rectangular baking dish. Sprinkle with ½ cup of the pecans.

2. Arrange half of the bread slices in a single layer in the baking dish. Sprinkle with ½ cup of the pecans; top with the remaining bread slices.

3. In a medium bowl whisk together eggs, milk, and vanilla. Gradually pour egg mixture over bread; press lightly with the back of a large spoon to moisten bread. In a small bowl stir together granulated sugar, cinnamon, and nutmeg; sprinkle over bread. Cover and chill for 2 to 24 hours.

4. Preheat oven to 350°F. Bake, uncovered, for 30 to 40 minutes or until lightly browned. Let stand for 10 minutes before serving. To serve, invert French toast onto a large serving platter. If desired, serve with raspberries, maple syrup, and/or additional pecans.

Per serving (2 slices): 579 cal., 27 g total fat (10 g sat. fat), 193 mg chol., 579 mg sodium, 72 g carbo., 3 g fiber, 15 g pro.

Caramel-Pecan French Toast

Cinnamon-Almond Ring

If the powdered sugar for the icing is lumpy, send it through the sifter or a fine-mesh sieve before using.

Prep: 45 minutes **Rise:** 1¾ hours
Bake: 50 minutes **Oven:** 350°F **Makes:** 16 servings

5½	to 6 cups all-purpose flour
2	packages active dry yeast
1	cup milk
½	cup water
½	cup butter, cut up
3	tablespoons sugar
1	teaspoon salt
2	eggs, lightly beaten
2	teaspoons finely shredded lemon peel
2	teaspoons finely shredded orange peel
1¼	cups sliced almonds, lightly toasted
6	tablespoons butter, softened
⅔	cup sugar
1	tablespoon ground cinnamon
1	recipe Powdered Sugar Icing

1. In a large bowl combine 2 cups of the flour and the yeast. In a saucepan heat and stir milk, water, the ½ cup butter, the 3 tablespoons sugar, and salt just until warm (120°F to 130°F) and butter almost melts. Add milk mixture to flour mixture along with the eggs, lemon peel, and orange peel. Beat with an electric mixer on low to medium for 30 seconds. Beat on high for 3 minutes. Using a spoon, stir in 1 cup of the sliced almonds and as much of the remaining flour as you can.

2. Turn dough out onto a lightly floured surface. Knead in enough of the remaining flour to make a moderately soft dough that is smooth and elastic (3 to 5 minutes total). Shape dough into a ball. Place dough in a lightly greased bowl, turning once to grease dough. Cover; let rise in a warm place until nearly double in size (about 1 hour). Punch dough down. Turn out onto a lightly floured surface. Cover; let rest 10 minutes. Meanwhile, lightly grease a 10-inch fluted tube pan; set aside.

3. For filling, in a bowl combine the 6 tablespoons softened butter, the ⅔ cup sugar, and cinnamon.

4. Roll dough into a 20×12-inch rectangle. Spread filling over dough to within ½ inch of edges. Roll up rectangle, starting from a long side. Seal seam. Place dough, seam side down, in pan. Bring ends together to form a ring. Cover; let rise in a warm place until nearly double in size (45 minutes).

5. Preheat oven to 350°F. Bake for 50 minutes or until golden, covering with foil the last 15 minutes of baking to prevent overbrowning. Invert tube pan onto a wire rack. Remove bread from pan and cool thoroughly. Drizzle with Powdered Sugar Icing and sprinkle with the remaining ¼ cup of the almonds.

Powdered Sugar Icing: In a small bowl combine 1 cup powdered sugar and ¼ teaspoon vanilla. Stir in enough milk (1 to 2 tablespoons) to make icing of drizzling consistency.

Perserving: 378 cal., 15 g total fat (7 g sat. fat), 54 mg chol., 234 mg sodium, 54 g carbo., 3 g fiber, 8 g pro.

Cherry Coffee Cake

This is one of those recipes with which you can be creative. Feel free to substitute peach, apricot, or raspberry preserves for the cherry preserves—the results will be equally delicious.

Prep: 25 minutes **Stand:** 45 minutes
Bake: 30 minutes **Cool:** 30 minutes **Oven:** 375°F
Makes: 12 to 16 servings

    Nonstick cooking spray
1 package 2-layer-size yellow cake mix
1 cup all-purpose flour
⅔ cup warm water (120°F to 130°F)
2 eggs
1 package active dry yeast
⅓ cup butter, melted
⅓ cup sliced almonds
1 teaspoon ground cinnamon
1 12-ounce jar cherry preserves
1 recipe Icing

1. Lightly coat a 13×9×2-inch baking pan with cooking spray; set aside. In a large mixing bowl combine 1½ cups of the cake mix, flour, water, eggs, and yeast. Beat with an electric mixer on low just until combined. Beat on medium for 2 minutes, scraping sides of bowl occasionally (mixture will be thick).

2. Spread batter into prepared pan; cover loosely and let stand at room temperature for 45 minutes.

3. Preheat oven to 375°F. For streusel, in a medium bowl stir together the remaining cake mix, melted butter, almonds, and cinnamon until combined. Spoon preserves in small mounds evenly over batter in pan. Crumble the streusel evenly over preserves.

4. Bake 30 minutes or until top is golden brown. Remove from oven; cool in pan on a wire rack for 30 minutes. Drizzle with icing. Serve warm.

Icing: In a small bowl stir together ¾ cup powdered sugar, 2 teaspoons lemon juice, and enough water (1 to 2 teaspoons) to make drizzling consistency. Drizzle over warm cake.

Per serving: 389 cal., 11 g total fat (5 g sat. fat), 49 mg chol., 338 mg sodium, 71 g carbo., 4 g pro.

Gingerbread Cinnamon Rolls

When cleaning up, remember to soak the dough bowl in cold—not hot—water. Hot water "cooks" the dough onto the bowl and makes it much more difficult to wash.

Prep: 30 minutes **Rise:** 1¾ hours
Bake: 22 minutes **Stand:** 15 minutes **Oven:** 350°F
Makes: 12 rolls

2 packages active dry yeast
½ cup evaporated milk
⅓ cup molasses
¼ cup packed brown sugar
1 egg, lightly beaten
2 tablespoons vegetable oil
4 cups all-purpose flour
¼ cup packed brown sugar
2 tablespoons granulated sugar
1 teaspoon ground cinnamon
½ teaspoon ground ginger
2 tablespoons butter, softened
1 recipe Spiced Glaze
    Sugared cranberries*

1. In a bowl combine yeast and ¼ cup warm water (about 115°F). Let stand 5 minutes. Stir in milk, molasses, ¼ cup brown sugar, egg, oil, and ½ teaspoon salt. Stir in as much flour as you can. Turn dough out onto floured surface. Knead in enough remaining flour for moderately soft, smooth, elastic dough (5 minutes). Shape into a ball. Place in greased bowl; turn once. Cover; let rise until double (1 hour). Punch down. Turn onto lightly floured surface. Cover; let rest 10 minutes.

2. Meanwhile, grease a 13×9×2-inch pan. For filling, in a bowl combine the ¼ cup brown sugar, granulated sugar, cinnamon, and ginger. Roll dough to 12×8-inch rectangle. Spread butter on dough. Sprinkle filling to within 1 inch along one long side. Roll up, beginning at long side of filling. Pinch to seal. Cut 12 slices. Place in pan. Cover; let rise until nearly double (45 minutes).

3. Preheat oven to 350°F. Bake for 22 to 25 minutes or until golden brown. Let stand 5 minutes; invert onto platter. Drizzle with Spiced Glaze. To serve, top with sugared cranberries.

Gingerbread Cinnamon Rolls

Spiced Glaze: In medium bowl combine 1½ cups powdered sugar, ½ teaspoon ground cinnamon, and ½ teaspoon vanilla. Whisk in enough milk (4 to 5 teaspoons total) to make drizzling consistency. Makes about ½ cup.

*Note: To make sugared cranberries, roll frozen cranberries in sugar.

Per rolls: 332 cal., 6 g total fat (2 g sat. fat), 26 mg chol., 136 mg sodium, 64 g carbo., 1 g fiber, 6 g pro.

Maple Sausage Corn Muffins

These savory muffins make a perfect accompaniment to scrambled eggs—but they're also sensational at supper served with cheese soup or tomato bisque.

Prep: 20 minutes **Bake:** 13 minutes
Cool: 5 minutes **Oven:** 425°F **Makes:** 18 muffins

- 1 **cup all-purpose flour**
- 1 **cup yellow cornmeal**
- 2 **tablespoons packed brown sugar**
- 1 **tablespoon baking powder**

- 1 **teaspoon dry mustard**
- ½ **teaspoon salt**
- 2 **large eggs, beaten**
- ½ **cup milk**
- ½ **cup pure maple syrup**
- ¼ **cup butter, melted**
- 8 **ounces cooked smoked sausage, chopped (about 1½ cups)**

1. Preheat oven to 425°F. Lightly grease fifteen 2½-inch muffin cups or line with paper bake cups.

2. In a bowl combine flour, cornmeal, brown sugar, baking powder, dry mustard, and salt. In a medium bowl whisk together eggs, milk, syrup, and butter. Add egg mixture all at once to flour mixture. Stir just until moistened. Stir in sausage. Spoon batter into muffin cups, filling each two-thirds full.

3. Bake for 13 to 15 minutes or until a wooden toothpick inserted near centers comes out clean. Cool in muffin cups on a wire rack for 5 minutes. Remove muffins from pans. Serve warm.

Per muffin: 156 cal., 7 g total fat (4 g sat. fat), 36 mg chol., 239 mg sodium, 19 g carbo., 1 g fiber, 4 g pro.

Banana Crunch Muffins

Use super-ripe bananas to achieve the most fantastic flavor in these family-favorite muffins.

Prep: 25 minutes **Bake:** 16 minutes
Cool: 5 minutes **Oven:** 375°F **Makes:** 12 muffins

¼	cup all-purpose flour
¼	cup granulated sugar
2	tablespoons butter
¼	cup chopped pecans
2	cups all-purpose flour
½	cup granulated sugar
⅓	cup packed brown sugar
1½	teaspoons baking soda
¼	teaspoon salt
¼	teaspoon ground cinnamon
¼	teaspoon ground nutmeg
½	cup butter
1	egg
1	cup mashed bananas (2 medium)
⅓	cup milk

Banana Crunch Muffins

1. Preheat oven to 375°F. Grease twelve 2½-inch muffin cups or line with paper bake cups; set aside. For topping, in a bowl stir together the ¼ cup flour and the ¼ cup granulated sugar. Using a pastry blender, cut in the 2 tablespoons butter until mixture resembles coarse crumbs. Stir in pecans.

2. In a medium bowl stir together the 2 cups flour, the ½ cup granulated sugar, the brown sugar, baking soda, salt, cinnamon, and nutmeg. Using a pastry blender, cut in the ½ cup butter until mixture resembles coarse crumbs. Make a well in the center of the flour mixture; set aside.

3. In a small bowl beat egg with a fork; stir in bananas and milk. Add egg mixture to flour mixture all at once; stir just until moistened (batter should be lumpy). Spoon batter into the prepared muffin cups, filling each three-fourths full. Sprinkle topping evenly over batter.

4. Bake for 16 to 18 minutes or until golden and a wooden toothpick inserted in the centers comes out clean. Cool in muffin cups on a wire rack for 5 minutes. Remove muffins from cups.

Per muffin: 285 cal., 12 g total fat (7 g sat. fat), 44 mg chol., 285 mg sodium, 42 g carbo., 1 g fiber, 2 g pro.

Granola

Consider making a double batch of this healthful breakfast treat—it makes a great gift for the whole grain lovers on your holiday gift list.

Prep: 15 minutes **Bake:** 30 minutes **Oven:** 300°F
Makes: about 7 cups (fourteen ½-cup servings)

2	cups regular rolled oats
1	cup coarsely chopped slivered or sliced almonds, chopped walnuts, or chopped pecans
½	cup flaked coconut (optional)
½	cup dry-roasted sunflower kernels
¼	cup toasted wheat germ
¼	cup flaxseed meal
½	cup honey or maple-flavored syrup
2	tablespoons vegetable oil

Granola

2 **teaspoons ground cinnamon (optional)**
1 **cup dried fruit (raisins, tart red cherries, blueberries, cranberries, and/or apricots, snipped) (optional)**

1. Preheat oven to 300°F. Grease a 15×10×1-inch baking pan; set aside. In a large bowl combine the oats, nuts, coconut (if using), sunflower kernels, wheat germ, and flaxmeal. Stir together honey, oil, and, if using; cinnamon; stir into oat mixture. Spread evenly in prepared pan.

2. Bake for 30 to 35 minutes or until lightly browned, stirring after 20 minutes. Remove from oven. If desired, stir in dried fruit.

3. Spread on a large piece of foil to cool. Store in an airtight container for up to 5 days. (Or store in freezer bags and freeze for up to 2 months.)

Per serving: 198 cal., 10 g total fat (1 g sat. fat), 0 mg chol., 2 mg sodium, 24 g carbo., 4 g fiber, 6 g pro.

Fruit-and-Nut Baked Oatmeal

Oven-baked oatmeal? What a clever way to free yourself from that last-minute stirring and fuss.

Prep: 15 minutes **Bake:** 20 minutes **Oven:** 350°F
Makes: 4 servings

1¾ cups milk
  2 tablespoons butter
  1 cup regular rolled oats
  ⅓ cup snipped dried apricots
  ⅓ cup dried tart cherries
  ⅓ cup golden raisins
  5 tablespoons packed brown sugar
  ½ teaspoon vanilla
  ¼ teaspoon salt
  ½ cup coarsely chopped pecans or walnuts
     Dried fruit (optional)
     Milk (optional)

1. Preheat oven to 350°F. In a medium saucepan bring 1¾ cups milk and butter to boiling. Slowly stir in oats. Stir in apricots, cherries, raisins, 3 tablespoons of the brown sugar, vanilla, and salt. Cook and stir for 1 minute. Pour into a lightly greased 1½-quart casserole.

2. Bake, uncovered, for 15 minutes. Sprinkle with the remaining 2 tablespoons brown sugar and nuts. Bake about 5 minutes more or until bubbly. Cool slightly. If desired, serve with additional dried fruit and milk.

Per serving: 446 cal., 19 g total fat (6 g sat. fat), 24 mg chol., 242 mg sodium, 63 g carbo., 5 g fiber, 9 g pro.

Brunch Baked Apples with Greek Yogurt

Greek yogurt is celebrated for its thick, creamy texture, which is comparable to sour cream.

Prep: 30 minutes **Bake:** 1 hour **Oven:** 350°F
Makes: 6 to 8 servings

  6 to 8 medium baking apples (such as McIntosh, Rome Beauty, or Granny Smith)
  1 cup orange juice
  1 cup rolled oats
  ½ cup packed brown sugar
  ⅓ cup slivered almonds, toasted
  1 tablespoon all-purpose flour
  ¾ teaspoon ground cinnamon
  ¼ teaspoon ground nutmeg
  ⅓ cup butter, melted
     Cinnamon sticks, broken (optional)
  ⅓ cup honey
  1 6- to 7-ounce carton Greek yogurt or other creamy-style yogurt

1. Preheat oven to 350°F. Remove a ½-inch slice from the top of each apple. Using a melon baller, remove cores, stopping about ½ inch from the bottom of the apple. Arrange apples in an ungreased 3-quart rectangular baking dish. (If necessary, remove a thin slice from the bottoms of the apples so they sit flat.) Brush with 1 tablespoon of the orange juice.

Brunch Baked Apples with Greek Yogurt

2. In a bowl combine oats, brown sugar, almonds, flour, ground cinnamon, and nutmeg. Stir in melted butter. Fill and top apples with oat mixture. Pour the remaining orange juice around apples.

3. Bake, covered, for 50 minutes. If desired, place pieces of cinnamon stick in oat mixture to resemble stems. Bake, uncovered, for 10 to 15 minutes more or until apples are tender. Cool slightly. Drizzle apples with honey. Serve with yogurt.

Per serving: 487 cal., 18 g total fat (9 g sat. fat), 32 mg chol., 89 mg sodium, 78 g carbo., 7 g fiber, 8 g pro.

Peach Sunrise Refresher

The summery taste of peaches is especially welcome during the cool holiday months. This beverage is as healthful as it is delicious.

Start to Finish: 5 minutes **Makes:** 4 servings

  2 **cups crushed ice**
1⅓ **cups pomegranate juice**
1⅓ **cups peach nectar**
    Mint sprigs (optional)
    Small orange wedges (optional)

1. Place ½ cup ice in each of 4 glasses. Add ⅓ cup of the pomegranate juice to each glass. Slowly fill each glass with ⅓ cup of the peach nectar. If desired, garnish each serving with mint sprigs and orange wedges.

Per serving: 95 cal., 0 g total fat, 0 mg chol.,9 mg sodium, 24 g carbo., 0 g fiber, 0 g pro.

Peach Sunrise Refresher

Strawberry-Mango Smoothies

To choose a juicy-ripe mango, look for unblemished yellow skin that is blushed with red.

Start to Finish: 10 minutes
Makes: 6 (6-ounce) servings

  2 **cups fresh strawberries, halved and chilled**
  1 **cup chopped fresh pineapple**
 ¾ **cup chopped bottled or fresh mango**
 ⅓ **cup unsweetened pineapple juice**
  2 **cups ice cubes**
    Fresh strawberries (optional)

1. In a blender combine strawberries, pineapple, mango, and pineapple juice. Cover and blend until smooth. With blender running, gradually add ice cubes through opening in lid. Blend until smooth after each addition. Serve immediately in chilled glasses. If desired, garnish each serving with strawberries.

Per serving: 48 cal., 0 g total fat, 0 mg chol., 1 mg sodium, 12 g carbo., 2 g fiber, 1 g pro.

seasonal breads

There is no time like Christmas to indulge in the joy of baking bread. The fruits of your labors—fragrant aromas, made-by-Mom flavors, and happy eaters—make your efforts so worthwhile. This assortment of tender-rich scones, crumbly coffee cakes, and lovely loaves is just right for your bread basket.

Orange-Raisin Brunch Bread, page 76

Chocolate-Pecan Coffee Cake

Chocolate-Pecan Coffee Cake

To quickly soften a stick of butter, remove it from the refrigerator and cut it into 8 or 10 chunks. Once cut, butter will reach its ideal creaming temperature in just 15 minutes.

Prep: 30 minutes **Bake:** 65 minutes
Cool: 50 minutes **Oven:** 350°F **Makes:** 12 servings

½	**cup butter, softened**
1	**cup granulated sugar**
2	**teaspoons baking powder**
½	**teaspoon baking soda**
½	**teaspoon kosher salt or ¼ teaspoon salt**
2	**eggs**
1	**teaspoon vanilla**
2¼	**cups all-purpose flour**
1	**8-ounce carton sour cream**
1	**recipe Coconut-Pecan Topping**

1. Preheat oven to 350°F. Grease and flour a 9-inch springform pan; set aside. In a large mixing bowl beat butter with an electric mixer on medium to high for 30 seconds. Add the sugar, baking powder, baking soda, and salt. Beat until well combined, scraping sides of bowl occasionally. Add eggs, one at a time, beating well after each addition. Beat in vanilla. Alternately add flour and sour cream to butter mixture, beating on low after each addition just until combined.

2. Spread half of the cake batter into prepared pan. Sprinkle with half of the Coconut-Pecan Topping. Spoon remaining cake batter in mounds over coconut mixture. Carefully spread to an even layer. Sprinkle with remaining Coconut-Pecan Topping.

3. Bake for 65 to 75 minutes or until a long wooden skewer inserted near the center comes out clean. If necessary, cover cake with foil for the last 15 to 20 minutes of baking to prevent overbrowning. Cool on wire rack for 20 minutes. Run a thin metal spatula around edge of cake. Remove sides of the pan. Cool 30 minutes more. Serve warm.

Coconut-Pecan Topping: In a large bowl combine 1 cup all-purpose flour, 1 cup packed brown sugar, and 1 teaspoon ground cinnamon. Cut in ½ cup cold butter until mixture resembles coarse crumbs; stir in ¾ cup semisweet chocolate pieces, ½ cup flaked coconut, and ½ cup chopped pecans.

Per serving: 561 cal., 29 g total fat (16 g sat. fat), 85 mg chol., 325 mg sodium, 71 g carbo., 3 g fiber, 6 g pro.

Apricot Coffee Cake

Apricots—bright and sunny little fruits that they are—add a most delectable cheer to this tender cake.

Prep: 25 minutes **Bake:** 35 minutes **Oven:** 350°F
Makes: 12 to 15 servings

1¾	cups all-purpose flour
1	teaspoon baking powder
½	teaspoon baking soda
¼	teaspoon salt
½	cup butter, softened
1	8-ounce package cream cheese, softened
1¼	cups granulated sugar
2	eggs, lightly beaten
1	teaspoon almond extract or vanilla
¼	cup milk
½	cup all-purpose flour
½	cup packed brown sugar
2	teaspoons ground cinnamon
¼	cup butter
½	cup chopped walnuts or almonds
1	24- to 26-ounce jar apricot halves, drained and halved into quarters

1. Preheat oven to 350°F. Grease and flour a 13×9×2-inch baking pan; set aside. In a medium bowl combine the 1¾ cups flour, baking powder, baking soda, and salt; set aside.

2. In a large mixing bowl beat ½ cup butter and cream cheese with an electric mixer on medium for 30 seconds. Add granulated sugar. Beat on medium to high until light and fluffy. Add eggs and almond extract; beat well. Alternately add flour mixture and milk to beaten egg mixture, beating until smooth after each addition.

3. Spread batter into prepared pan. Bake for 25 to 30 minutes or until top is lightly browned. Meanwhile, in a small bowl combine the ½ cup flour, brown sugar, and ground cinnamon. Cut in butter until mixture resembles coarse crumbs. Stir in walnuts. Carefully arrange quartered apricots on top of cake. Sprinkle nut mixture over cake.

4. Bake for 10 to 15 minutes more or until a toothpick inserted near the center comes out clean. Serve warm.

Per serving: 445 cal., 22 g total fat (12 g sat. fat), 87 mg chol., 279 mg sodium, 57 g carbo., 2 g fiber, 4 g pro.

Apricot Coffee Cake

Honey-Glazed Buttermilk Oatmeal Coffee Cake

Don't let its lengthy ingredient list deter you from baking this superlative special-day delicacy.

Prep: 30 minutes Bake: 25 minutes
Cool: 10 minutes Oven: 375°F Makes: 9 servings

½ cup honey
⅓ cup butter, melted
2 tablespoons light-color corn syrup
2 teaspoons finely shredded lemon peel
4 teaspoons lemon juice
½ cup chopped pecans
1½ cups rolled oats
1 cup all-purpose flour
¾ cup packed brown sugar
½ cup chopped pecans
1 teaspoon baking powder
½ teaspoon baking soda
½ teaspoon salt
⅔ cup buttermilk
2 eggs, lightly beaten
¼ cup butter, melted
1½ teaspoons vanilla

1. Preheat oven to 375°F. Grease a 9×9×2-inch baking pan. In a small bowl combine ½ cup honey, ⅓ cup melted butter, corn syrup, lemon peel, and lemon juice. Stir in ½ cup chopped pecans. Pour into prepared pan; set aside.

2. For cake, in a blender or food processor blend or process oats until finely ground. Transfer to a large bowl. Stir in flour, brown sugar, ½ cup pecans, baking powder, baking soda, and salt. Make a well in the center of the dry ingredients. In a medium bowl combine buttermilk, eggs, ¼ cup melted butter, and vanilla. Add the milk mixture all at once to the flour mixture. Stir just until moistened (batter should be lumpy).

3. Spoon batter evenly over honey mixture. Bake for 25 minutes or until a wooden toothpick inserted in center comes out clean. Remove from oven and immediately invert cake onto a serving plate. Cool about 10 minutes. Serve warm.

Per serving: 450 cal., 23 g total fat (9 g sat. fat), 79 mg chol., 357 mg sodium, 58 g carbo., 3 g fiber, 6 g pro.

Pumpkin-Praline Muffins

Be sure that you purchase solid canned pumpkin— not pumpkin pie filling—for these magnificent holiday muffins.

Prep: 20 minutes Bake: 20 minutes
Cool: 5 minutes Oven: 375°F Makes: 12 muffins

⅓ cup packed brown sugar
2 tablespoons sour cream
⅔ cup chopped pecans, toasted
2 cups all-purpose flour
2 teaspoons baking powder
1 teaspoon ground cinnamon
½ teaspoon baking soda
¼ teaspoon salt
¼ teaspoon ground nutmeg
⅛ teaspoon ground cloves
1 egg
¾ cup buttermilk
¾ cup canned pumpkin
⅔ cup packed brown sugar
⅓ cup butter, melted

1. Preheat oven to 375°F. Grease twelve 2½-inch muffin cups or line with paper bake cups; set aside. For topping, in a small bowl stir together the ⅓ cup brown sugar and the sour cream; stir in pecans. Set aside.

2. In a medium bowl stir together the flour, baking powder, cinnamon, baking soda, salt, nutmeg, and cloves. Make a well in the center of the flour mixture; set aside. In another medium bowl lightly beat egg with a fork; stir in buttermilk, pumpkin, the ⅔ cup brown sugar, and the melted butter. Add pumpkin mixture to flour mixture all at once; stir just until moistened (batter should be lumpy). Spoon batter into the prepared muffin cups, filling each three-quarters full. Spoon topping evenly over batter.

3. Bake for 20 to 25 minutes or until golden brown. Cool in muffin cups on a wire rack for 5 minutes. Remove muffins from cups. Serve warm.

Per muffin: 250 cal., 11 g total fat (4 g sat. fat), 32 mg chol., 215 mg sodium, 36 g carbo., 2 g fiber, 2 g pro.

Double Chocolate Scones

Double Chocolate Scones

Dutch-process cocoa powder undergoes a process that neutralizes cocoa's natural acidity. It is a bit darker and richer than regular unsweetened cocoa, and either form will work well in these sensational scones.

Prep: 20 minutes Bake: 12 minutes Oven: 400°F
Makes: 12 scones

- 2 **cups all-purpose flour**
- ½ **cup granulated sugar**
- ⅓ **cup unsweetened European-style (Dutch-process) cocoa powder or unsweetened cocoa powder**
- 1 **tablespoon baking powder**
- ½ **teaspoon salt**
- ⅓ **cup unsalted butter**
- 1 **beaten egg**
- ½ **cup whipping cream**
- 1 **teaspoon vanilla**
- 1 **cup miniature semisweet chocolate pieces**
- ½ **cup chopped pecans, toasted (optional)**
  Whipping cream (optional)
  Coarse sugar (optional)

1. Preheat oven to 400°F. Line a large baking sheet with parchment paper; set aside. In a large bowl stir together flour, granulated sugar, cocoa powder, baking powder, and salt. Using a pastry blender, cut in the butter until mixture resembles coarse crumbs. Make a well in the center of flour mixture.

2. In a bowl stir together egg, ½ cup whipping cream, and vanilla. Add egg mixture to flour mixture all at once. Add chocolate pieces and, if desired, the pecans. Using a fork, stir until just moistened.

3. Turn dough out onto a lightly floured surface. Knead dough by folding and gently pressing it for 10 to 12 strokes or until dough is nearly smooth. (Handle dough as little as possible to keep it light.) Divide dough in half. Pat or lightly roll half the dough into a 4½-inch circle, about 1 inch thick. Cut into 6 wedges. Repeat with remaining dough. Place wedges 1 inch apart on the prepared baking sheet. If desired, brush wedges with additional whipping cream and sprinkle with coarse sugar.

4. Bake for 12 to 14 minutes or until bottoms are lightly browned. Remove scones from baking sheet. Serve warm.

Per scone: 312 cal., 15 g total fat (9 g sat. fat), 46 mg chol., 207 mg sodium, 39 g carbo., 1 g fiber, 5 g pro.

Fresh Cranberry Scones

The spunky taste of cranberries is too terrific to limit to the holiday months. Pop a bag or two in the freezer so you can enjoy them throughout the year.

Prep: 20 minutes **Bake:** 20 minutes **Oven:** 375°F
Makes: 8 scones

2¼	cups all-purpose flour
2	tablespoons sugar
1	tablespoon baking powder
¼	teaspoon salt
1½	cups fresh cranberries, finely chopped*
2	tablespoons honey
1	cup whipping cream
1	egg, lightly beaten
1	tablespoon water
1	tablespoon sugar

1. Preheat oven to 375°F. In a large bowl stir together the flour, 2 tablespoons sugar, the baking powder, and salt. Make a well in the center of the flour mixture; set aside.

2. In a medium bowl stir together the cranberries and honey; stir in whipping cream. Add cranberry mixture to flour mixture all at once. Using a fork, stir just until moistened.

3. Turn dough out onto a lightly floured surface. Knead dough by folding and gently pressing it for 10 to 12 strokes or until dough is nearly smooth. Dough may appear pink. Pat or lightly roll dough into an 8-inch circle. Cut into 8 wedges. Place wedges about 1 inch apart on an ungreased baking sheet. In a small bowl stir together the egg and water. Lightly brush wedges with egg mixture and sprinkle with 1 tablespoon sugar.

4. Bake for 20 to 25 minutes or until tops are golden brown. Remove scones from baking sheet; serve warm.

***Note:** To finely chop cranberries, place them in a food processor. Cover and pulse several times.

Per scone: 300 cal., 12 g total fat (7 g sat. fat), 68 mg chol., 184 mg sodium, 42 g carbo., 2 g fiber, 6 g pro.

Fresh Cranberry-Orange Scones: Prepare as above, except stir 1½ teaspoons finely shredded orange peel into the cranberry mixture. For icing, combine 1 cup powdered sugar, 1 tablespoon orange juice, and ¼ teaspoon vanilla; stir in additional orange juice, 1 teaspoon at a time, to make drizzling consistency. Drizzle over scones.

Fresh Cranberry-Bittersweet Scones: Prepare as above, except stir ⅔ cup (3 ounces) coarsely chopped bittersweet chocolate into the cranberry mixture. For icing, drizzle 2 ounces melted bittersweet chocolate over scones.

Fresh Cranberry-Pecan Scones: Prepare as above, except stir ⅔ cup coarsely chopped toasted pecans into the cranberry mixture. For icing, in a small bowl combine 1 cup powdered sugar, 2 tablespoons maple syrup, and ¼ teaspoon vanilla. Stir in milk, 1 teaspoon at a time, to make icing smooth and drizzling consiceny. Drizzle over scones.

Fresh Cranberry Scones

Tomato Pesto Scones with Kalamata Olives

Kalamta olives are a Greek variety prized for their deep eggplant-color flesh and rich, almost fruity flavor.

Prep: 25 minutes **Bake:** 12 minutes **Oven:** 425°F
Makes: 9 to 15 scones

- 1 cup dried tomatoes (not oil-packed) (3 ounces)
- 2 cups all-purpose flour
- 1 0.5-ounce envelope pesto sauce mix
- 2 teaspoons baking powder
- ½ teaspoon baking soda
- ¼ cup butter
- ¾ cup milk
- 1 egg yolk
- ½ cup pitted kalamata olives, coarsely chopped and drained
- 1 tablespoon snipped fresh rosemary
- 1 tablespoon olive oil
  Rosemary sprigs

1. In a bowl combine dried tomatoes and enough boiling water to cover. Let stand for 10 minutes; drain. Remove two of the dried tomatoes; set aside. Chop remaining tomatoes and set aside.

2. Preheat oven to 425°F. Line a large baking sheet with parchment paper; set aside. In a large bowl combine flour, pesto sauce mix, baking powder, and baking soda. Using a pastry blender, cut in butter until mixture resembles coarse crumbs. Make a well in the center of the flour mixture.

3. In a medium bowl combine milk and egg yolk. Add egg mixture all at once to flour mixture. Stir in the chopped tomatoes, olives, and snipped rosemary just until combined.

4. Turn dough out onto a lightly floured surface. Knead dough by folding and gently pressing it for 10 to 12 strokes or just until dough holds together. With floured hands, pat or lightly roll dough to a 9×6-inch rectangle on prepared baking sheet. Using a sharp knife, cut scones into 9 to 15 diamond-shape pieces (do not separate.) Lightly press the

Tomato Pesto Scones with Kalamata Olives

reserved tomatoes and a few rosemary sprigs into top of dough. Brush with olive oil. Bake for 12 to 14 minutes or until lightly browned. Gently pull or cut scones to separate. Serve warm.

Per scone: 208 cal., 9 g total fat (4 g sat. fat), 39 mg chol., 595 mg sodium, 27 g carbo., 2 g fiber, 5 g pro.

Prosciutto Biscuits

2. Make a well in center of flour mixture; add milk all at once. Using a fork, stir just until moistened. Turn dough out onto a lightly floured surface. Knead dough by folding and gently pressing 4 to 6 strokes or just until dough holds together. Lightly roll dough to 9×5-inch rectangle. Using a long knife or pizza cutter, cut dough lengthwise in half, then crosswise in fourths, making 8 rectangles.

3. Arrange dough pieces on ungreased baking sheet. Bake 12 to 14 minutes or until biscuits are golden brown. Remove from baking sheet and serve warm.

Note: To make ahead, prepare as at left through Step 1. Place flour mixture in airtight storage container. Cover and refrigerate up to 3 days. To suse, let stand at room temperature for 10 minutes. Continue as directed in Step 2. Bake time may increase by 1 to 2 minutes.

Per biscuit: 187 cal., 11 g total fat (7 g sat. fat), 31 mg chol., 368 mg sodium, 16 g carbo., 1 g fiber, 5 g pro.

Prosciutto Biscuits

Sharp provolone is a cheese worth looking for. Although sometimes available in half-moons or slices, the best are wax-dipped spheres that hang from lengths of braided string.

Prep: 20 minutes **Bake:** 12 minutes **Oven:** 425°F
Makes: 8 biscuits

1⅓ cups all-purpose flour
   1 teaspoon baking powder
   1 teaspoon fennel seeds, crushed
   ½ teaspoon sugar
   ¼ teaspoon salt
   ¼ teaspoon baking soda
   6 tablespoons cold butter, cut up
   ½ cup sharp provolone or cheddar cheese, shredded (2 ounces)
   ⅓ cup thinly sliced prosciutto or cooked ham, finely chopped (1 cup)
   ½ cup milk

1. Preheat oven to 425°F. In a medium bowl stir together flour, baking powder, fennel seeds, sugar, salt, and baking soda. Using a pastry blender, cut in butter until flour mixture resembles coarse crumbs. Stir in cheese and prosciutto.

Biscuits with Berry-Cherry Filling

Pure maple syrup has a highly nuanced sweetness that inexpensive pancake syrups lack. Splurge for the real stuff if you can—its flavor is divine.

Prep: 20 minutes **Bake:** 25 minutes **Oven:** 375°F
Makes: 12 biscuits

   1 22- to 26-ounce package frozen unbaked biscuits (12)
   ⅔ cup dried cranberries
   ⅔ cup dried cherries
   ⅔ cup pure maple syrup
   1 teaspoon fresh thyme leaves
      Cayenne pepper (optional)
      Pure maple syrup

1. Prepare biscuits according to package directions until golden. Remove from oven and cool slightly.

2. Meanwhile, in a food processor combine cranberries, cherries, the ⅔ cup maple syrup, and thyme. Cover and process until mixture is a coarse paste. If desired, add cayenne pepper to taste.

3. Using a fork, carefully split the warm biscuits horizontally. Spread a rounded tablespoon of the fruit mixture onto bottom half of each biscuit. Replace biscuit tops. Brush with additional maple syrup. Bake for 5 minutes more. Serve warm.

Per biscuit: 344 cal., 9 g total fat (3 g sat. fat), 0 mg chol., 608 mg sodium, 60 g carbo., 2 g fiber, 5 g pro

Easy Florentine Rolls

The term "Florentine" is a French word that refers to spinach-containing dishes prepared in the style of Florence, Italy.

Prep: 25 minutes **Bake:** 18 minutes
Stand: 2 minutes **Oven:** 375°F **Makes:** 12 rolls

- 4 **green onions, finely chopped**
- 2 **cloves garlic, minced**
- 2 **tablespoons olive oil**
- 1 **6-ounce package fresh baby spinach**
- ¼ **cup snipped fresh basil**
- ½ **teaspoon salt**
- ¼ **teaspoon black pepper**
- 1 **13.8-ounce package refrigerated pizza dough**

- ¼ **cup crumbled feta cheese (1 ounce)**
- 2 **tablespoons toasted pine nuts**
- 1 **tablespoon butter, melted**
- ¼ **cup finely shredded Parmesan cheese**

1. Preheat oven to 375°F. Grease twelve 2½-inch muffin cups; set aside. In a large skillet cook green onions and garlic in 1 tablespoon of the oil until tender. Add spinach and basil; cook and stir over medium heat just until wilted. Drain off excess liquid. Stir in salt and pepper. Set aside to cool.

2. On a well-floured surface, unroll pizza dough and shape into a 12×8-inch rectangle. Brush surface of dough with the remaining 1 tablespoon oil. Spread spinach mixture to within 1 inch of the edges of dough. Sprinkle with feta cheese and pine nuts. Starting with one of the long sides, roll dough into a spiral.

3. Slice roll into 12 pieces. Place, cut sides up, in prepared muffin cups. Brush with butter and sprinkle with Parmesan cheese. Bake for 18 to 20 minutes or until golden brown. Let stand for 2 minutes. Carefully remove from cups. Serve warm.

Per roll: 165 cal., 9 g total fat (4 g sat. fat), 13 mg chol., 443 mg sodium, 14 g carbo., 1 g fiber, 7 g pro.

Easy Florentine Rolls

Potato Pancetta Galette

Pancetta is an Italian bacon that is cured with salt and spices but not smoked. This full-flavored meat comes in rounds rather than strips.

Prep: 25 minutes **Bake:** 12 minutes **Oven:** 400°F
Makes: 12 servings

- 6   ounces pancetta, cut into ¼-inch cubes; or bacon, finely chopped; or finely chopped ham
      Cornmeal
- 1   13.8-ounce package refrigerated pizza dough
- 4   ounces tiny new red potatoes
- 2   tablespoons olive oil
- 1   tablespoon fresh thyme leaves
- ¼   teaspoon freshly ground black pepper
- ⅓   cup finely shredded Asiago cheese

1. In a large skillet cook pancetta on medium heat until crisp and brown. Drain on paper towels; set aside.

2. Preheat oven to 400°F. Grease a large baking sheet; sprinkle with cornmeal. Unroll pizza dough onto baking sheet. Slice potatoes into ¹⁄₁₆-inch-thick slices. Arrange potato slices on dough. Brush generously with olive oil; sprinkle with thyme and pepper. Top with pancetta and cheese. Bake for 12 to 15 minutes or until crust is golden brown and potatoes are tender. To serve, cut to make 6 pieces; halve pieces diagonally.

Per serving: 142 cal., 8 g total fat (2 g sat. fat), 10 mg chol., 312 mg sodium, 14 g carbo., 1 g fiber, 4 g pro.

Oatmeal Batter Bread

No need to knead? What a brilliant idea!

Prep: 25 minutes **Rise:** 45 minutes
Bake: 40 minutes **Oven:** 350°F
Makes: 1 loaf (12 slices)

- 1   cup warm milk (105°F to 115°F)
- ¼   cup honey or packed brown sugar
- 1   package active dry yeast
- 1¾ cups all-purpose flour
- 1   egg, lightly beaten
- 1   tablespoon cooking oil
- ½   teaspoon salt
- ¾   cup whole wheat flour
- ½   cup rolled oats

1. In a bowl combine milk, honey, and yeast; stir until yeast dissolves. Let stand for 5 minutes. Grease an 8×4×2-inch loaf pan; set aside.

2. Add flour, egg, oil, and salt to yeast mixture. Beat with an electric mixer on low until combined. Beat for 3 minutes on high. Stir in whole wheat flour and oats until combined. Spoon batter into prepared loaf pan. Cover; let dough rise in a warm place until double in size (about 45 minutes).

3. Preheat oven to 350°F. Bake for 40 minutes or until bread sounds hollow when lightly tapped. If necessary, cover bread with foil the last 10 minutes of baking to prevent overbrowning. Immediately remove bread from pan. Cool on wire rack.

Per slice: 166 cal., 3 g total fat (1 g sat. fat), 19 mg chol., 113 mg sodium, 31 g carbo., 2 g fiber, 5 g pro.

Potato Pancetta Galette

Oatmeal Batter Bread

Cheese Straws

Frozen puff pastry—miracle of the modern kitchen—makes these tasty sticks absolutely foolproof.

Prep: 20 minutes **Bake:** 15 minutes **Oven:** 375°F
Makes: 32 to 36 cheese straws

1⅓ **cups grated Parmesan cheese**
  2 **teaspoons fennel seeds**
  1 **teaspoon mustard seeds**
  1 **teaspoon poppy seeds**
  1 **teaspoon caraway seeds**
  ½ **teaspoon black sesame seeds**
  ½ **teaspoon white sesame seeds**
  ½ **teaspoon garlic powder**
  ½ **teaspoon black pepper**
  ¼ **teaspoon salt**
  ¼ **teaspoon ground turmeric**
  ¼ **teaspoon paprika**
  ⅛ **teaspoons cayenne pepper**
  1 **egg, lightly beaten**
  3 **tablespoons water**
  1 **package frozen puff pastry sheets, thawed (2 sheets)**

1. Preheat oven to 375°F. Line two baking sheets with parchment paper; set aside.

2. In a mixing bowl combine cheese, fennel seeds, mustard seeds, poppy seeds, caraway seeds, black and white sesame seeds, garlic powder, pepper, salt, turmeric, paprika, and cayenne pepper. Set aside. In a small bowl beat together egg and water.

3. On a lightly floured cutting board, unfold one sheet of puff pastry. Brush the surface lightly with some of the egg mixture. Top with half of the cheese mixture to evenly cover entire surface. Roll a floured rolling pin over cheese to gently press the cheese into the puff pastry.

4. Cut the puff pastry into long ½-inch-wide strips; gently twist each strip several times. Lay strips 1 inch apart on a prepared baking sheet. Repeat with remaining sheet of puff pastry, egg mixture, and cheese mixture. Bake for 15 minutes or until the straws are golden in color. Cool on wire rack. They are best served the same day but can be stored overnight in an airtight container.

Per cheese straw: 130 cal., 7 g total fat (2 g sat. fat), 9 mg chol., 109 mg sodium, 7 g carbo., 0 g fiber, 3 g pro.

Flax Soda Bread

Mild and nutty-tasting flaxseeds are a rich source of health-enhancing omega-3 fatty acids. It is available in the health food section of most grocery stores.

Prep: 25 minutes **Bake:** 30 minutes **Oven:** 375°F
Makes: 12 to 16 servings

- 1   cup unbleached all-purpose flour
- ¾   cup whole wheat flour or rye flour
- ½   cup ground flaxseeds
- ¾   teaspoon baking powder
- ½   teaspoon baking soda
- ½   teaspoon salt
- 3   tablespoons butter
- 2   eggs, lightly beaten
- ¾   cup buttermilk or sour milk*
- 2   tablespoons honey
- ¼   cup flaxseeds
- 1   egg, lightly beaten

1. Preheat oven to 375°F. Lightly grease a baking sheet; set aside. In a large bowl stir together all-purpose flour, whole wheat flour, ground flaxseeds, baking powder, baking soda, and salt. Using a pastry blender, cut in butter until mixture resembles coarse crumbs. Make a well in the enter of the flour mixture; set aside.

2. In a small bowl stir together the 2 eggs, buttermilk, and honey. Add egg mixture to flour mixture all at once. Using a fork, stir just until moistened. Stir in flaxseeds. (Dough will be sticky.)

3. Turn dough out onto a well-floured surface. With well-floured hands, knead dough by folding and gently pressing it for 10 to 12 strokes or until dough is nearly smooth. On the prepared baking sheet, pat the dough into a 7-inch oval loaf. With a sharp knife, cut a 4-inch cross, ¼ inch deep, on top of the loaf. Lightly brush with the remaining egg.

4. Bake for 30 to 35 minutes or until a wooden toothpick inserted near the center comes out clean. Remove bread from baking sheet; serve warm.

*Note: To make sour milk, place 1½ teaspoons lemon juice or vinegar in a glass measuring cup. Add enough milk to equal ½ cup liquid. Let mixture stand for a few minutes before using.

Per serving: 166 cal., 7 g total fat (3 g sat. fat), 16 mg chol., 227 mg sodium, 20 g carbo., 3 g fiber, 6 g pro.

Flax Soda Bread

Three-Grain Rolls

If you use rye flour infrequently, be sure to store it in an airtight bag in the freezer. Measure the amount you need and allow it to come to room temperature before using.

Prep: 45 minutes **Rise:** 1½ hours
Rest: 10 minutes **Bake:** 12 minutes
Oven: 375°F **Makes:** 24 rolls

- 2 **cups warm water (105°F to 115°F)**
- 2 **packages active dry yeast**
- 1 **teaspoon sugar**
- ½ **cup sugar**
- ½ **cup cooking oil**
- 2 **eggs, lightly beaten**
- 1½ **teaspoons salt**
- 1 **cup rye flour**
- ½ **cup regular rolled oats**
- ½ **cup whole bran cereal**
- 4¼ **to 4¾ cups all-purpose flour**

1. In a large mixing bowl combine 1 cup of the warm water, the yeast, and the 1 teaspoon sugar. Let stand for 5 minutes or until yeast dissolves and mixture is bubbly on top. Using a wooden spoon, stir the remaining 1 cup warm water, the ½ cup sugar, oil, eggs, and salt into yeast mixture. Add rye flour, oats, and bran cereal, stirring to combine. Let stand for 5 minutes.

2. Add 2 cups of the all-purpose flour to the yeast mixture. Beat with an electric mixer on low to medium for 30 seconds, scraping sides of bowl constantly. Beat on high for 3 minutes. Using the wooden spoon, stir in as much of the remaining all-purpose flour as you can.

3. Turn dough out onto a lightly floured surface. Knead in enough of the remaining flour to make a moderately stiff dough that is smooth and elastic (8 to 10 minutes total). Dough may be sticky. Shape dough into a ball. Place dough in a lightly greased bowl, turning once to grease surface. Cover; let dough rise in a warm place until double in size (about 1 hour).

4. Punch dough down. Turn out onto a lightly floured surface. Cover; let rest for 10 minutes. Meanwhile, grease two large baking sheets or twenty-four 2½-inch muffin cups; set aside.

Three-Grain Rolls

5. Shape dough into 24 balls. Place balls 2½ inches apart on prepared baking sheets or in prepared muffin cups. Cover; let rolls rise in a warm place until nearly double in size (about 30 minutes).

6. Preheat oven to 375°F. Bake for 12 minutes or until golden brown. Immediately remove rolls from baking sheets or muffin cups. Cool on wire racks.

Per roll: 172 cal., 6 g total fat (1 g sat. fat), 18 mg chol., 156 mg sodium, 27 g carbo., 2 g fiber, 4 g pro.

Orange-Raisin Brunch Bread

Orange-Raisin Brunch Bread

*Orange zest brightens this stunning bread beautifully.
Add a colorful ribbon to create an edible wreath for
gift giving.*

Prep: 30 minutes **Rise:** 1 hour 40 minutes
Rest: 5 minutes **Bake:** 25 minutes **Oven:** 350°F
Makes: 8 to 10 servings

- 2¾ to 3¼ cups all-purpose flour
- 1 package active dry yeast
- ½ cup butter
- ¼ cup milk
- ¼ cup water
- 2 tablespoons sugar
- ½ teaspoon salt
- 2 eggs
- 1 tablespoon finely shredded orange peel
- ¾ cup golden raisins
  Milk
- 1 recipe Powdered Sugar Icing
  Apricot jam

1. In a large mixing bowl combine 1½ cups flour
and yeast; set aside.

2. In medium saucepan heat butter, the ¼ cup milk,
water, sugar, and salt on medium heat until very
warm (120°F to 130°F) and butter almost melts.
Add butter mixture, eggs, and orange peel to flour
mixture. Beat on low until combined; beat on high
3 minutes. With a wooden spoon, stir in raisins and
as much remaining flour as you can.

3. Turn out dough on lightly floured surface.
Knead in enough remaining flour for moderately
soft dough that is smooth and elastic (3 to
5 minutes). Place in greased bowl; turn to grease
surface. Cover; let rise in warm place 1 hour or
until nearly doubled in size.

4. Punch dough down; turn onto work surface.
Cover; let rest 5 minutes. Equally divide dough in
three; roll each to a 26-inch length. Lay side by
side 1 inch apart; braid. Pinch each end of braid
together. Transfer to large greased baking sheet.

Shape in ring and pinch both ends together. Cover with plastic wrap; let rise 40 minutes, dough will rise slightly.

5. Preheat oven to 350°F. Lightly brush bread ring with milk. Place a foil ball or ovensafe glass measure or jar in center to preserve shape. Bake 25 to 30 minutes or until golden and bread sounds hollow when tapped. Remove from oven; cool. Place on platter and drizzle with Powdered Sugar Icing. Cut into slices and serve with apricot jam.

Powdered Sugar Icing: In a small bowl combine 1 cup powdered sugar and ¼ teaspoon vanilla. Stir in enough milk (1 to 2 tablespoons) to make icing drizzling consistency.

Per serving: 343 cal., 13 g total fat (8 g sat. fat), 84 mg chol., 252 mg sodium, 49 g carbo., 2 g fiber, 4 g pro.

Pumpkin Rolls with Maple Streusel Filling

Maple sugar can be purchased from many online specialty baking companies.

Prep: 1 hour Rise: 1½ hours
Rest: 10 minutes Bake: 12 minutes per batch
Oven: 375°F Makes: 16 rolls

4½ to 5 cups all-purpose flour
 1 package active dry yeast
 ½ cup milk
 ½ cup water
 ¼ cup butter
 ¼ cup sugar
 ¾ teaspoon salt
 1 egg, beaten
 ½ cup canned pumpkin
 1 recipe Maple Streusel

1. In a large mixing bowl combine 1½ cups of the flour and yeast; set aside. In a medium saucepan heat milk, water, butter, sugar, and salt just until warm (120°F to 130°F) and butter almost melts. Add milk mixture to flour mixture along with egg. Beat with an electric mixer on low to medium for 30 seconds, scraping sides of bowl constantly. Beat on high for 3 minutes. Beat in canned pumpkin.

Using a wooden spoon, stir in as much of the remaining flour as you can.

2. Turn dough out onto a lightly floured surface. Knead in enough of the remaining flour to make a moderately stiff dough that is smooth and elastic (6 to 8 minutes total). Shape dough into a ball. Place in a large greased bowl, turning once to grease surface of the dough. Cover and let rise in a warm place until nearly double in size (about 1 hour). Or cover and chill overnight (dough will rise overnight).

3. Punch dough down. Turn dough out onto a lightly floured surface. Divide dough in half. Cover and let rest for 10 minutes. Meanwhile, lightly grease two large baking sheets and prepare Maple Streusel.

4. Divide each half of dough into 8 equal portions. On a lightly floured surface, flatten each piece into a 3½-inch round. Spoon 1 tablespoon of the Maple Streusel in the center of each round. Shape the dough into a round ball by pulling the edges of dough up and over streusel, pinching edges of dough to seal. Place rolls, smooth sides up, about 2 inches apart on prepared baking sheets. Cover and let rise in a warm place until nearly double in size (30 to 40 minutes). Preheat oven to 375°F.

5. Bake rolls, one pan at a time, for 12 to 14 minutes or until golden brown. Immediately transfer rolls to wire racks. Serve warm.

Maple Streusel: In a medium bowl stir together ⅔ cup chopped hazelnuts (filberts) or pecans, ⅓ cup maple sugar or packed brown sugar, ⅓ cup all-purpose flour, and ¼ cup snipped dried apricots. Stir in ⅓ cup melted butter until combined.

Make-ahead directions: Prepare rolls a day ahead and store at room temperature in an airtight container. Or place cooled rolls in plastic freezer storage bags and freeze up to 3 weeks. To serve, wrap room-temperature rolls in foil or thaw frozen rolls overnight at room-temperature and wrap in foil. Heat wrapped rolls in a 325°F oven about 15 minutes or until warm.

Per roll: 273 cal., 11 g total fat (5 g sat. fat), 32 mg chol., 166 mg sodium, 38 g carbo., 2 g fiber, 6 g pro.

joyful desserts

If you believe that the best holiday traditions come out of the oven, this chapter is for you. Choose any of these divine desserts—whether you pick a featherlight cake, airy meringue pie, silky-smooth custard, dense cheesecake, or rustic bread pudding, it will end any festive dinner on a sweet note.

Coconut Meringue Cheesecake, page 91

Orange-Rosemary Pound Cake

rack. If desired, serve cake with berries and additional sour cream and garnish with fresh rosemary sprigs.

Per serving: 190 cal., 7 g total fat (3 g sat. fat), 39 mg chol., 149 mg sodium, 30 g carbo., 0 g fiber, 3 g pro.

White Chocolate Layer Cake with Cranberry Filling

When you make this luscious cake be sure to choose high-quality white chocolate—those varieties that list cocoa butter on the ingredients list are best.

Prep: 45 minutes **Chill:** 2 hours **Bake:** 30 minutes
Cool: 30 minutes **Stand:** 30 minutes **Oven:** 350°F
Makes: 16 servings

- 1 12-ounce package fresh cranberries
- 1¼ cups granulated sugar
- ¼ cup cranberry juice
- 2 teaspoons finely shredded orange peel
- 2 teaspoons lemon juice
- ¼ teaspoon ground cinnamon
- ⅛ teaspoon ground ginger
- ⅛ teaspoon ground cloves
- 8 ounces white baking chocolate, chopped
- 2¼ cups all-purpose flour
- 2¼ teaspoons baking powder
- ¼ teaspoon salt
- 10 tablespoons butter, softened
- 1⅓ cups granulated sugar
- 4 eggs
- 1½ teaspoons vanilla
- 1¼ cups milk
- 12 ounces white baking chocolate, chopped
- 1 cup butter, softened
- 2 teaspoons vanilla
- 2 cups powdered sugar
- 1 recipe Sugared Cranberries (optional)
  Mint leaves (optional)

1. For filling, in a saucepan combine cranberries, the 1¼ cups granulated sugar, cranberry juice, orange peel, lemon juice, cinnamon, ginger, and cloves. Bring to boiling; reduce heat. Simmer, uncovered, about 10 minutes or until thickened. Transfer filling to a medium bowl. Cover and chill for 2 hours. Transfer to a blender or food processor. Cover and blend or process until smooth.

Orange-Rosemary Pound Cake

Fresh rosemary infuses a doctored-up cake mix with fresh, sohisticated flavor.

Prep: 15 minutes **Bake:** 45 **Stand:** 10 minutes
Cool: 2 hours **Oven:** 350°F
Makes: 12 to 14 servings

- 1 16-ounce package pound cake mix
- ½ cup sour cream
- 2 eggs
- ⅓ cup water
- 1½ teaspoons finely shredded orange peel
- 1 teaspoon snipped fresh rosemary
  Raspberries or blueberries (optional)
  Sour cream (optional)
  Fresh rosemary sprigs (optional)

1. Preheat oven to 350°F. Grease and lightly flour a 9×5×3-inch loaf pan. Set aside.

2. In a large bowl combine cake mix, sour cream, eggs, and water. Beat with an electric mixer on low for 30 seconds. Beat on medium for 3 minutes. Stir in orange peel and snipped rosemary.

3. Pour batter evenly into the prepared pan. Bake for 45 to 55 minutes or until a wooden toothpick inserted near the center of cake comes out clean. Cool cake in pan on a wire rack for 10 minutes. Remove cake from pan; cool completely on wire

2. Meanwhile, preheat oven to 350°F. Grease the bottoms of two 9×1½-inch round cake pans. Line bottoms of pans with waxed paper; grease and lightly flour pans. Set aside.

3. In a medium saucepan cook and stir the 8 ounces white chocolate on low heat until melted. In a medium bowl combine flour, baking powder, and salt; set aside. In a large bowl beat the 10 tablespoons butter with an electric mixer on medium to high for 30 seconds. Gradually add the 1⅓ cups granulated sugar, beating until combined. Add eggs one at a time, beating after each addition. Beat in the 1½ teaspoons vanilla. Alternately add flour mixture and milk to butter mixture, beating on low after each addition just until combined. Beat in melted white chocolate just until combined. Spread batter in the prepared cake pans.

4. Bake about 30 minutes or until a toothpick inserted in the centers comes out clean. Cool cake layers in pans on wire racks for 10 minutes. Remove layers from pans. Peel off waxed paper. Cool completely on wire racks.

5. For frosting, in a medium saucepan cook and stir the 12 ounces white chocolate on low heat until melted. Cool for 20 minutes. In a large bowl beat the 1 cup butter on medium to high until fluffy. Beat in melted white chocolate and the 2 teaspoons vanilla. Gradually beat in powdered sugar.

6. To assemble, use a long serrated knife to cut each cake layer in half horizontally. Place one layer, cut side up, on a serving plate. Spread with one-third of the filling. Top with the second layer; spread with one-third of the filling. Top with the third layer; spread with the remaining filling. Top with the fourth layer, cut side down.

7. Spread top and sides of cake with frosting. If desired, cover loosely and chill up to 24 hours. Let stand about 30 minutes at room temperature before serving, if chilled. If desired, top with sugared cranberries and mint leaves.

Per serving: 648 cal., 32 g total fat (3 g sat. fat), 111 mg chol., 274 mg sodium, 87 g carbo., 2 g fiber, 6 g pro.

Sugared Cranberries: Roll frozen cranberries in granulated sugar.

White Chocolate Layer Cake with Cranberry Filling

Turtle Cake

When baking with cooking oil, choose a mild-flavor oil such as canola or safflower oil.

Prep: 30 minutes **Bake:** 25 minutes
Chill: 1 hours **Cool:** 2 hours **Oven:** 350°F
Makes: 12 to 16 servings

	Unsweetened cocoa powder
1	egg, slightly beaten
1	cup buttermilk or sour milk*
⅔	cup cooking oil
2	cups all-purpose flour
1¾	cups sugar
½	cup unsweetened cocoa powder
1	tablespoon baking soda
1	teaspoon salt
1	cup freshly brewed hot coffee
1	recipe Chocolate Frosting
1½	cups pecan halves, toasted
¾	cup purchased caramel ice cream topping

1. Preheat oven to 350°F. Grease three 9-inch cake pans. Line the bottom of each pan with parchment paper. Grease the paper; dust with unsweetened cocoa powder. Set pans aside.

2. In a small bowl stir together egg, buttermilk, and cooking oil; set aside. In a large mixing bowl stir together flour, sugar, ½ cup cocoa powder, baking soda, and salt. Gradually add buttermilk mixture to flour mixture, beating with an electric mixer until combined. Gradually beat in hot coffee. Pour batter into prepared pans; spread evenly. (Layers will appear shallow.)

3. Bake for 25 to 30 minutes or until a wooden toothpick inserted near the centers comes out clean. Cool cakes on wire racks for 10 minutes. Loosen sides from pans, then invert cakes on racks. Remove cakes from pans. Peel off paper; cool thoroughly.

4. When the cakes are cool, make the Chocolate Frosting. Place one cake layer, top side down, onto a serving plate. Using an icing spatula or wide knife, work quickly to frost the top of this layer with one-third of the frosting, pushing it out slightly from edges to make ripple or petal effect. Arrange one-third of the pecans on top and drizzle with ¼ cup of the ice cream topping. Top with the second layer, top side down. Repeat with frosting, pecans, and caramel topping. Top with the third layer, right side up. Repeat with remaining frosting, pecans, and caramel topping.

5. Chill cake 1 to 2 hours before serving.

Chocolate Frosting: In a small saucepan combine 1 cup sugar and ½ cup milk. Add 6 tablespoons butter. Bring to boiling, stirring constantly. Remove from heat. Add one 12-ounce package (2 cups) semisweet chocolate pieces. Using a wire whisk, mix until smooth. If frosting is too thick or grainy, stir in 1 to 2 teaspoons freshly brewed hot coffee. Makes about 2½ cups.

*Note: To make sour milk, place 1 tablespoon lemon juice or vinegar in a glass measuring cup. Add enough milk to equal 1 cup total liquid; stir. Let mixture stand for 5 minutes before using.

Per serving: 716 cal., 37 g total fat (10 g sat. fat), 35 mg chol., 639 mg sodium, 97 g carbo., 4 g fiber, 8 g pro.

Turtle Cake

Molten Chocolate Cakes with Cherry Compote

To chill the molten filling more quickly, transfer the chocolate mixture to a shallow baking dish before covering and refrigerating.

Prep: 80 minutes **Chill:** 1 hour **Bake:** 15 minutes
Stand: 10 minutes **Oven:** 375°F **Makes:** 8 servings

- 1⅓ **cups semisweet chocolate pieces**
- 1 **tablespoon butter**
- ½ **cup whipping cream**
- 4 **ounces semisweet chocolate, coarsely chopped**
- ½ **cup butter**
- 4 **eggs**
- ½ **cup sugar**
- ½ **cup all-purpose flour**
- 1 **recipe Cherry Compote**
  Vanilla ice cream (optional)

1. Generously butter eight 6-ounce ramekins. For filling: In a small saucepan combine chocolate pieces, the 1 tablespoon butter, and the whipping cream. Cook and stir on low heat until chocolate is melted and mixture is smooth. Cool at room temperature for 15 minutes. Cover and chill in the refrigerator for 1 to 2 hours or until fudgelike in consistency.

2. Preheat oven to 375°F. In a small saucepan combine chopped semisweet chocolate and the ½ cup butter. Cook and stir on low heat until chocolate is melted and mixture is smooth. Cool slightly.

3. In a large bowl combine eggs and sugar; beat with an electric mixer on medium-high for 5 minutes. Beat in flour and melted chocolate mixture. Spoon enough of the batter into each ramekin to measure 1 inch in depth.

4. Divide chilled filling into 8 portions. Working quickly, use your hands to roll each portion into a ball. Place a ball of filling on top of the batter in each ramekin; do not allow the filling to touch ramekin sides. Divide remaining batter among ramekins.

Molten Chocolate Cakes with Cherry Compote

5. Bake for 15 minutes. Remove from oven; let stand at room temperature for 10 minutes. Using a paring knife, loosen sides; invert onto serving plates. Serve immediately with warm Cherry Compote. If desired, serve with vanilla ice cream.

Cherry Compote: In a small saucepan combine 1 cup orange juice and ½ teaspoon finely shredded orange peel. Bring just to boiling on medium heat. In a small bowl combine ¼ cup sugar and 1 tablespoon cornstarch. Stir sugar mixture into orange juice mixture. Return to boiling. Cook and stir for 2 minutes more. Remove from heat. Stir in 1½ cups pitted fresh or thawed frozen sweet cherries and, if desired, 2 tablespoons cherry brandy or brandy. Allow to cool slightly before serving.

Bake-ahead directions: Prepare as directed through Step 4. Cover and chill up to 4 hours. Bake and serve as directed in Step 5.

Per serving: 547 cal., 34 g total fat (20 g sat. fat), 161 mg chol., 136 mg sodium, 60 g carbo., 4 g fiber, 6 g pro.

Malibu Rum Baby Cakes

Malibu Rum Baby Cakes

If you prefer baking without spirits, substitute ¼ cup orange juice for the rum and add ½ teaspoon rum flavoring.

Prep: 45 minutes **Bake:** 25 minutes
Cool: 5 minutes **Oven:** 350°F **Makes:** 6 servings

1	8-ounce can pineapple slices (juice pack)
¼	cup Malibu rum or light rum
¼	cup dried apricots, quartered
3	tablespoons butter
½	cup packed brown sugar
	Nonstick cooking spray for baking
1⅓	cups all-purpose flour
¼	cup flaked coconut
2	teaspoons baking powder
¼	cup butter, softened
½	cup granulated sugar
1	egg
	Sweetened whipped cream (optional)

1. Drain pineapple well, reserving liquid (you should have about ⅓ cup juice). Set pineapple slices aside. In a small saucepan combine reserved pineapple juice, rum, and apricots. Bring the mixture just to boiling; remove from heat. Let stand for 15 minutes. Strain, reserving both the liquid and the apricots. In the same saucepan combine the 3 tablespoons butter, the brown sugar, and 1 tablespoon of the reserved liquid. Cook and stir on medium heat until butter is melted and sugar is dissolved.

2. Lightly coat the insides of six 10-ounce ramekins or custard cups or six 1-cup fluted tube pans with nonstick cooking spray. Spoon the brown sugar mixture evenly into the prepared pans. Cut each pineapple slice into 6 pieces. Arrange pineapple and apricots evenly on top of the sugar mixture. Set aside.

3. Preheat oven to 350°F. In a small bowl stir together flour, coconut, and baking powder; set aside. Measure the remaining juice mixture; add enough water to equal ⅔ cup; set aside.

4. In a medium mixing bowl beat the ¼ cup butter with an electric mixer on medium to high for 30 seconds. Add granulated sugar and beat until light and fluffy. Add egg and beat until combined. Alternately add the ⅔ cup liquid and the flour mixture, beating on low after each addition just until combined.

5. Carefully spoon batter over fruit in ramekins. Bake about 25 minutes or until tops spring back when lightly touched. Cool in ramekins on wire racks for 5 minutes. Loosen cakes from ramekins; invert cakes onto serving plates. Serve warm. If desired, top with whipped cream.

Per serving: 446 cal., 16 g total fat (10 g sat. fat), 71 mg chol., 212 mg sodium, 67 g carbo., 2 g fiber, 2 g pro.

Orange-Pistachio Cassata Torte

Cassata is a special occasion cake often served at Italian weddings and other celebrations.

Prep: 1½ hours **Bake:** 45 minutes
Cool: 1½ hour **Chill:** overnight
Oven: 350°F **Makes:** 16 servings

1	10.75-ounce frozen pound cake, thawed and sliced ¼ inch thick
3	tablespoons orange liqueur
2	8-ounce cartons mascarpone cheese
1	cup whole milk ricotta cheese
¾	cup sugar

3 tablespoons all-purpose flour

3 eggs

½ cup snipped Candied Orange Peel or purchased candied orange peel

1 cup chopped pistachio nuts

12 ounces bittersweet chocolate, chopped

1 cup whipping cream

1 tablespoon sugar

1 teaspoon orange liqueur
Candied Orange Peel or purchased candied orange peel

1. Preheat oven to 350°F. Drizzle cake slices with the 3 tablespoons orange liqueur. Arrange some of the slices around the side of a 9-inch springform pan, overlapping as needed. Arrange remaining cake slices on bottom of pan, cutting to fit.

2. In a large mixing bowl beat mascarpone cheese, ricotta cheese, the ¾ cup sugar, and the flour with an electric mixer on medium until smooth. Beat in eggs just until combined. Stir in the ½ cup Candied Orange Peel, ⅓ cup of the pistachio nuts, and ⅓ cup of the chocolate. Pour into prepared pan.

3. Bake for 45 minutes or until outer 1½ inches of filling is set. Cool in pan on a wire rack for 30 minutes. Remove sides of pan. Cool for 1 hour.

4. In a small saucepan heat ⅓ cup of the cream just until bubbly. Remove from heat; add remaining chocolate. Let stand for 5 minutes; stir until chocolate is melted. Spread sides of torte with some of the chocolate mixture. Press remaining ⅔ cup pistachio nuts onto sides. Carefully spread the remaining chocolate over the top of the torte. If necessary, spread with the back of a spoon. Cover loosely and chill overnight.

5. Let torte stand at room temperature for 30 minutes before serving. Just before serving, in a small chilled mixing bowl beat the remaining ⅔ cup cream, the 1 tablespoon sugar, and the 1 teaspoon orange liqueur with an electric mixer on medium to high until soft peaks form (tips curl). Garnish torte with additional Candied Orange Peel and serve with whipped cream.

Per serving: 511 cal., 36 g total fat (20 g sat. fat), 133 mg chol., 90 mg sodium, 43 g carbo., 3 g fiber, 13 g pro.

Candied Orange Peel: Cut peels of 2 medium oranges lengthwise into quarters, cutting just through the pulp to the surface of the fruit. Pry back the quartered peel using the back of the spoon. Scrape away the pith (the soft white part inside the peel). If the pith is left on, the peel will be bitter. Cut peel into ¼-inch-wide strips. Wrap and refrigerate peeled fruit for another use. In a 2-quart saucepan combine 1⅓ cups sugar and ⅓ cup water. Bring to boiling, stirring constantly. Add orange peel strips. Return to boiling; reduce heat. Simmer, uncovered, on medium-low heat about 15 minutes or until peel is almost translucent, stirring occasionally. Remove from heat. Using a slotted spoon, remove peel from syrup, allowing each spoonful to drain over the saucepan about 30 seconds. Transfer peel to a wire rack set over waxed paper. Set cooked peel aside until cool enough to handle but still warm and slightly sticky. Roll peel in additional sugar to coat. Continue drying on the rack for 1 to 2 hours. Store, tightly covered, in a cool, dry place for up to 1 week. Or freeze for up to 6 months. Makes about 2 cups.

Orange-Pistachio Cassata Torte

Polenta and Plum Cake

Polenta is Italian cornmeal. This rustic—and yet elegant—dessert is not too sweet and ends dinner on a delightful note.

Prep: 30 minutes **Bake:** 50 minutes **Cool:** 2 hours
Oven: 350°F **Makes:** 10 servings

4	plums, pitted and cut into wedges
¼	cup packed brown sugar
1	cup all-purpose flour
½	cup yellow cornmeal
1½	teaspoons baking powder
⅛	teaspoon salt
1	cup butter, softened
¾	cup granulated sugar
4	egg yolks
2	eggs
1	teaspoon finely shredded lemon or orange peel
1	teaspoon vanilla
	Whipped cream (optional)

1. Preheat oven to 350°F. Lightly grease and flour bottom and sides of a 9-inch springform pan; line bottom with a 9-inch circle of parchment paper. Arrange plums on parchment in pan. Sprinkle brown sugar over the plums. Set aside.

2. In a small bowl combine flour, cornmeal, baking powder, and salt; set aside.

3. In a large mixing bowl beat the butter with an electric mixer on medium to high for 30 seconds. Add granulated sugar and beat until light. Add egg yolks and eggs, one at a time, beating after each addition. Add lemon peel and vanilla; beat until combined. Beat in the flour mixture. Spoon batter over plums in pan and spread evenly.

4. Bake for 50 minutes or until a wooden toothpick inserted near center comes out clean. Cool cake in pan on a wire rack for 20 minutes. Remove sides of pan; cool cake completely. Invert cake onto serving platter; remove bottom of pan and parchment. If desired, serve with whipped cream.

Per serving: 356 cal., 21 g total fat (13 g sat. fat), 173 mg chol., 216 mg sodium, 37 g carbo., 1 g fiber, 4 g pro.

Polenta and Plum Cake

Lemon-Berry Ribbon Torte

When eggs are beaten at room temperature—as they are here—they give cake layers maximum loft and tenderness.

Prep: 40 minutes **Bake:** 20 minutes
Cool: 30 minutes **Chill:** 2 hours
Oven: 350°F **Makes:** 12 servings

3	eggs
1½	cups all-purpose flour
1½	teaspoons baking powder
1½	cups granulated sugar
¾	cup milk
3	tablespoons butter
	Powdered sugar
1	8-ounce carton sour cream
1	cup whipping cream
¾	cup powdered sugar
1	teaspoon vanilla
⅔	cup purchased lemon curd
⅔	cup raspberry preserves
	Small fresh lemon thyme or thyme sprigs (optional)
	Fresh raspberries (optional)

Lemon-Berry Ribbon Torte

1. Allow eggs to stand at room temperature for 30 minutes. Meanwhile, grease the bottom of a 15×10×1-inch baking pan; line with waxed paper. Grease and flour the waxed paper and sides of pan; set aside. In a small bowl, stir together flour and baking powder; set aside.

2. Preheat oven to 350°F. In a large bowl beat eggs with an electric mixer on high about 4 minutes or until thick. Gradually add granulated sugar, beating on medium for 4 to 5 minutes or until light and fluffy. Add the flour mixture; beat on low to medium just until combined.

3. In a small saucepan combine milk and butter; heat and stir until butter melts. Add milk mixture to egg-flour mixture; beat until combined. Pour batter into the prepared pan.

4. Bake for 20 to 25 minutes or until cake springs back when lightly touched. Immediately loosen edges of cake from pan; turn out onto a clean kitchen towel sprinkled with powdered sugar. Remove waxed paper. Cool completely. Cut cake crosswise into thirds; set aside.

5. For sour cream frosting, in a large bowl combine sour cream, whipping cream, the ¾ cup powdered sugar, and the vanilla. Beat with an electric mixer on medium until mixture thickens and holds stiff peaks. Place about 1 cup of the sour cream frosting into a pastry bag fitted with a small star tip.

6. To assemble, place one of the cake layers on a serving plate. Spread with lemon curd. Top with another cake layer; spread with raspberry preserves. Top with remaining cake layer. Frost top and sides of cake with the remaining sour cream frosting. Pipe a border around edges of cake. Cover and chill for 2 to 4 hours before serving.

7. If desired, place thyme sprigs in a pie plate; dust with powdered sugar. Place raspberries on a plate; dust with powdered sugar. Garnish cake with sugared thyme sprigs and raspberries.

Per serving: 458 cal., 17 g total fat (10 g sat. fat), 111 mg chol., 111 mg sodium, 74 g carbo., 10 g fiber, 3 g pro.

Ginger and Apple Sleds

Ginger and Apple Sled Tarts

Crystalized ginger—also called candied ginger—is gingerroot that has been cooked in a sugar syrup and then dusted with coarse sugar.

Prep: 25 minutes **Bake:** 20 minutes **Oven:** 400°F
Makes: 12 servings

- ½ **of a 17.3-ounce package frozen puff pastry sheets (1 sheet), thawed**
- 1 **egg, slightly beaten**
- 1 **tablespoon water**
- 2 **tablespoons coarse or granulated sugar**
- 2 **tablespoons finely chopped crystallized ginger**
- 2 **small baking apples, cored, halved, and thinly sliced**

1. Preheat oven to 400°F. Line a large baking sheet with parchment paper; set aside. Unfold pastry onto a lightly floured surface. Roll pastry into a 12-inch square. Place pastry square on prepared baking sheet. Cut in half to form 2 rectangles; separate slightly. Prick pastry rectangles all over with a fork.

2. In a small bowl combine the egg and water; brush pastry with the egg mixture. Fold in all edges of each rectangle about ¼ inch, pressing lightly as you fold to form a rim. Brush folded edges with egg mixture; set pastry aside.

3. In a small bowl stir together sugar and ginger. Arrange apple slices over pastry, overlapping as necessary. Sprinkle with sugar mixture.

4. Bake for 20 to 25 minutes or until pastry is deep golden brown and crisp. Cool on baking sheet on a wire rack. When cool, transfer to a cutting board or platter. Cut crosswise into rectangles.

Per serving: 120 cal., 7 g total fat (0 g sat. fat), 18 mg chol., 83 mg sodium, 14 g carbo., 1 g fiber, 1 g pro.

Chocolate Bread Pudding

Brioche and challah are egg-rich breads that possess light, almost cakelike texture.

Prep: 35 minutes **Chill:** 2 hours
Bake: 65 minutes **Cool:** 1 hour
Oven: 400°F/325°F **Makes:** 8 servings

- 8 ounces brioche or challah
- ⅓ cup unsalted butter, melted
- 1½ cups whipping cream
- ½ cup milk
- 6 ounces bittersweet or semisweet chocolate, finely chopped, or 1 cup semisweet chocolate pieces
- 6 egg yolks
- ⅓ cup granulated sugar
- 4 ounces bittersweet or semisweet chocolate, coarsely chopped
   Vanilla ice cream

1. Preheat oven to 400°F. Cut bread into ½-inch cubes (you should have about 6 cups). In a large bowl toss bread cubes with melted butter. Transfer buttered bread cubes to a shallow baking pan. Bake for 10 to 12 minutes or until golden brown, stirring once. Set aside.

2. In a medium saucepan combine whipping cream, milk, and the 6 ounces chocolate. Cook and stir on medium heat until chocolate is melted. In a large bowl, whisk together egg yolks and sugar. Gradually whisk cream mixture into egg yolks. Stir in toasted bread. Cover and refrigerate 2 hours or overnight.

3. Preheat oven to 325°F. Lightly butter a 2-quart square baking dish. Stir remaining 4 ounces chocolate into chilled bread mixture. Pour into prepared dish. Place dish in a roasting pan. Place pan on rack in oven. Pour boiling water into the roasting pan around baking dish to a depth of 1 inch. Bake, uncovered, for 55 minutes or until evenly puffed and top is set.

4. Carefully remove baking dish from water. Cool about 1 hour on a wire rack. Scoop into serving dishes. Serve with vanilla ice cream.

Per serving: 582 cal., 46 g total fat (26 g sat. fat), 268 mg chol., 190 mg sodium, 43 g carbo., 3 g fiber, 8 g pro.

Ginger-Pumpkin Meringue Pie

To crush cookies and crackers, place in a plastic bag and roll with a rolling pin until finely textured.

Prep: 30 minutes **Bake:** 69 minutes **Chill:** 2 hours
Oven: 375°F/350°F **Makes:** 8 servings

- 1 recipe Gingersnap-Graham Crust
- 1 15-ounce can pumpkin
- ⅓ cup sugar
- 1 teaspoon ground ginger
- ½ teaspoon salt
- ½ teaspoon ground cinnamon
- 3 eggs, lightly beaten
- ⅔ cup milk
- ½ cup maple syrup
- 1 recipe Brown Sugar Meringue

1. Preheat oven to 375°F. Prepare Gingersnap-Graham Crust; bake 4 minutes. Cool on wire rack.

2. For filling, in a bowl combine pumpkin, sugar, ginger, salt, and cinnamon. Add eggs; beat with a fork to combine. Stir in milk and maple syrup.

3. Pour filling into pastry shell. To prevent overbrowning, cover edge of pie with foil. Bake for 50 to 55 minutes or until knife inserted near center comes out clean. Uncover edges. Reduce oven to 350°F. Carefully spread Brown Sugar Meringue over hot filling; seal to edge. Bake 15 minutes or until golden brown. Cool on wire rack. Loosely cover and refrigerate within 2 hours.

Gingersnap-Graham Crust: In a large bowl combine ¾ cup finely crushed gingersnaps, ½ cup finely crushed graham crackers, and 2 tablespoons granulated sugar. Stir in ¼ cup melted butter. Spread evenly on bottom and up the sides of a 9-inch pie plate.

Brown Sugar Meringue: In a large mixing bowl let 3 egg whites stand at room temperature 30 minutes. Add ½ teaspoon vanilla, ¼ teaspoon cream of tartar, and ⅛ teaspoon salt. Beat on medium until soft peaks form. Gradually add ⅓ cup packed brown sugar, beating on high until mixture forms stiff peaks (tips stand straight).

Per serving: 316 cal., 10 g total fat (5 g sat. fat), 96 mg chol., 404 mg sodium, 52 g carbo., 2 g fiber, 6 g pro.

Cream Puffs

Light and airy cream puffs are the ballerinas of the dessert world. Prepare them early and pop them in the freezer—they'll be ready any time you need them.

Prep: 25 minutes **Cool:** 10 minutes
Bake: 30 minutes **Oven:** 400°F
Makes: 12 cream puffs

 1 **cup water**
 ½ **cup butter**
 ⅛ **teaspoon salt**
 1 **cup all-purpose flour**
 4 **eggs**
 3 **cups whipped cream, pudding, or ice cream**

1. Preheat oven to 400°F. Lightly grease a baking sheet; set aside. In a medium saucepan combine water, butter, and salt. Bring to boiling. Add flour all at once, stirring vigorously. Cook and stir until mixture forms a ball. Remove from heat. Cool for 10 minutes. Add eggs, one at a time, beating well with a wooden spoon after each addition.

2. Drop dough into 12 mounds onto prepared baking sheet. Bake for 30 to 35 minutes or until golden brown and firm. Transfer cream puffs to a wire rack to cool.

3. Cut off the top one-third of each cream puff; remove soft dough from inside. Fill with whipped cream. Replace tops.

Per cream puff: 238 cal., 21 g total fat (12 g sat. fat), 134 mg chol., 140 mg sodium, 9 g carbo., 0 g fiber, 4 g pro.

Chocolate Cream Puffs: Prepare as above, except add 2 tablespoons sugar to the saucepan with the water, butter, and salt. Stir 3 tablespoons unsweetened cocoa powder into the flour before adding the flour to the butter mixture.

Filling options: Scoop any flavor ice cream into each cut puff; replace top. Drizzle with hot fudge sauce. Spoon 1 tablespoon prepared chocolate pudding into each cut puff; replace top. Serve with chopped strawberries tossed with sugar. Spoon chopped fresh pineapple, chopped toasted macadamia nuts, and toasted coconut into each cut puff. Drizzle with caramel-flavor ice cream topping; replace top.

Festive Berry Trifle

Three ruby-color fruits help this pretty trifle get all dresssed up for Christmas.

Prep: 1 hour **Chill:** 10 hours **Makes:** 10 servings

 3 **cups cranberries**
 1½ **cups fresh or frozen raspberries**
 1½ **cups granulated sugar**
 1 **cup dried cherries (5 ounces)**
 1 **cup water**
 1 **tablespoon finely shredded orange peel**
 ½ **cup granulated sugar**
 2 **teaspoons cornstarch**
 ⅛ **teaspoon salt**
 2 **cups half-and-half or light cream**
 1 **vanilla bean, halved lengthwise and seeds scraped from pod, or 1 teaspoon vanilla**
 6 **egg yolks, lightly beaten**
 ½ **cup ruby Port**
 ¼ **cup granulated sugar**
 ¼ **cup water**
 2 **10 ¾-ounce frozen pound cakes, thawed**
 1 **4-ounce bar bittersweet chocolate, chopped**
 1 **cup whipping cream**
 2 **tablespoons powdered sugar**
    Bittersweet chocolate shavings (optional)

1. For berry filling, in a saucepan stir together the cranberries, raspberries, the 1½ cups granulated sugar, cherries, 1 cup water, and orange peel. Bring to boiling; reduce heat. Simmer, uncovered, about 15 minutes or until reduced to 4¼ cups, stirring occasionally. Chill, loosely covered, about 4 hours or until cold (filling thickens as it cools).

2. For vanilla custard, in a medium saucepan stir together the ½ cup granulated sugar, the cornstarch, and salt. Stir in half-and-half and vanilla seeds, if using, until smooth. Cook and stir on medium heat until slightly thickened and bubbly. Reduce heat; cook and stir 2 minutes more. Gradually stir about 1 cup of the hot mixture into egg yolks; return mixture to saucepan. Cook and stir 2 minutes more. Stir in vanilla, if using. Pour into a bowl. Cover and chill about 4 hours.

3. For Port syrup, in a small saucepan combine Port, the ¼ cup granulated sugar, and the ¼ cup water. Simmer, stirring occasionally, until sugar is dissolved. Let stand until room temperature.

Festive Berry Trifle

4. To assemble trifles, cut each cake horizontally into thirds. Brush both sides of each slice evenly with the Port syrup. Cut each slice into ¾-inch squares. Line the bottom of each of 10 glass trifle dishes with half the cake, overlapping pieces if necessary. Top with half of the berry mixture, half the custard, and half the chopped chocolate. Repeat layering. Cover and chill for 2 to 24 hours.

5. To serve, in a medium mixing bowl beat whipping cream with powdered sugar until soft peaks form. Spoon onto each trifle. If desired, garnish with chocolate shavings.

Per serving: 820 cal., 38 g total fat (21 g sat. fat), 298 mg chol., 329 mg sodium, 113 g carbo., 3 g fiber, 10 g pro.

Coconut Meringue Cheesecake

Coconut tends to go rancid quickly. Be sure to store any unused portion tightly wrapped in the refrigerator.

Prep: 30 minutes **Bake:** 55 minutes **Cool:** 1 hour
Chill: 4 hours **Oven:** 350°F/ 325°F
Makes: 12 servings

1½ cups shredded coconut
 ¼ cup finely chopped pecans
 2 tablespoons butter, melted
 2 8-ounce packages cream cheese, softened
 ⅓ cup sugar
 3 tablespoons unsweetened cocoa powder
 2 tablespoons milk
 1 teaspoon vanilla
 4 egg yolks
 ½ cup chopped pecans
 4 egg whites
 1 teaspoon vanilla
 ½ teaspoon cream of tartar
 ½ cup sugar
    Large shards fresh coconut, toasted, or
    flaked coconut, toasted

1. Preheat oven to 350°F. Grease the bottom and sides of an 8-inch springform pan; set aside. Combine the 1½ cups coconut and the ¼ cup pecans; stir in melted butter. Press coconut mixture firmly onto bottom of pan. Bake for 10 to 12 minutes or until lightly browned. Remove from oven.

2. Meanwhile, for filling, in a large bowl beat cream cheese with an electric mixer on medium until fluffy. Add the ⅓ cup sugar, the cocoa powder, milk, and 1 teaspoon vanilla. Beat until smooth. Beat in egg yolks just until combined (do not overbeat). Pour into crust-lined pan. Place springform pan in a shallow baking pan. Bake for 25 to 30 minutes or until center appears nearly set when shaken. Remove from oven; sprinkle with the ½ cup pecans.

3. Meanwhile, for meringue, thoroughly wash and dry beaters. In a large bowl combine egg whites, 1 teaspoon vanilla, and cream of tartar. Beat with electric mixer on medium about 1 minute or until soft peaks form (tips curl). Gradually add the ½ cup sugar, 1 tablespoon at a time, beating on high about 5 minutes or until stiff, glossy peaks form (tips stand straight).

4. Spread meringue over hot cheesecake, carefully sealing to edge of pan. Reduce oven temperature to 325°F. Return cheesecake to oven; bake for 30 minutes more.

5. Cool cheesecake in springform pan on a wire rack for 1 hour. Loosen and remove side of the springform pan. Cover and chill for 4 to 24 hours before serving. Before serving, sprinkle with toasted coconut.

Per serving: 413 cal., 32 g total fat (16 g sat. fat), 117 mg chol., 217 mg sodium, 28 g carbo., 2 g fiber, 7 g pro.

Peppermint Fudge Pie

Peppermint-Fudge Pie

This dynamite dessert is a lifesaver during the busy holiday season. Prepare and freeze it up to a month before you need it—it will be ready when you are.

Prep: 50 minutes **Bake:** 7 minutes
Freeze: 8 hours **Oven:** 375°F **Makes:** 12 servings

- 1 **recipe Chocolate Crumb Crust**
- 1 **cup sugar**
- 1 **5-ounce can (⅔ cup) evaporated milk**
- 2 **tablespoons butter**
- 2 **ounces unsweetened chocolate, cut up**
- 1 **teaspoon vanilla**
- 2 **pints (4 cups) peppermint ice cream**
- 1 **recipe Peppermint Whipped Cream**
  Crushed striped round peppermint candies
  (optional)

1. Prepare Chocolate Crumb Crust; set aside. For fudge sauce, in a small saucepan combine the 1 cup sugar, the evaporated milk, butter, and chocolate. Cook and stir on medium heat until bubbly; reduce heat. Boil gently for 4 to 5 minutes or until mixture is thickened and reduced to 1½ cups. Remove from heat; stir in vanilla. If necessary, beat until smooth with a wire whisk or rotary beater. Spread about half of the warm fudge sauce over the cooled Chocolate Crumb Crust; freeze until set. Set remaining fudge sauce aside.

2. In a chilled bowl stir peppermint ice cream until softened; spread over fudge sauce layer. Freeze about 2 hours or until set. Spread remaining fudge sauce evenly over ice cream. Top with Peppermint Whipped Cream. Freeze for at least 6 hours or until set. If desired, sprinkle with crushed peppermint candies just before serving.

Chocolate Crumb Crust: Preheat oven to 375°F. Lightly coat an 8-inch springform pan with nonstick cooking spray; set aside. In a bowl combine 1 cup finely crushed vanilla wafers, ⅓ cup powdered sugar, and 3 tablespoons unsweetened cocoa powder. Stir in 3 tablespoons butter, melted. Pat crust mixture firmly into the bottom of prepared pan. Bake for 7 to 8 minutes or until crust is firm. Cool in pan on a wire rack.

Peppermint Whipped Cream: In a chilled mixing bowl beat 1½ cups whipping cream with an electric mixer on medium until stiff peaks form; fold in ¼ cup crushed striped round peppermint candies (about 10).

Per serving: 439 cal., 26 g total fat (16 g sat. fat), 77 mg chol., 142 mg sodium, 49 g carbo., 1 g fiber, 4 g pro.

Banana Caramel Custard

When preparing the caramel, place sugar in a light-color skillet. If you use a dark one, you won't be able to see the caramel change color quite as well.

Prep: 40 minutes **Bake:** 1¼ hours
Cool: 2¼ hours **Chill:** overnight **Oven:** 350°F
Makes: 10 to 12 servings

1½	**cups sugar**
3	**cups eggnog**
6	**eggs**
2	**teaspoons vanilla**
⅛	**teaspoon salt**
2	**tablespoons butter**
⅛	**teaspoon ground cinnamon**
1	**to 2 ripe but firm bananas, sliced**
	¼ to ½ inch thick

1. Preheat oven to 350°F. Arrange rack in center of oven. For caramelized sugar, place ½ cup sugar in a heavy medium skillet, shaking to make an even layer. Heat on medium-high until some of the sugar is melted (it should look syrupy). Stir only the melted sugar to keep it from overbrowning, stirring in remaining sugar as it melts. Reduce heat to medium-low. Cook and stir until all the sugar is melted and golden. Quickly pour into the bottom of a 10-cup soufflé dish.

3. Meanwhile, for custard, in a large bowl whisk together remaining 1 cup sugar, eggnog, eggs, vanilla, and salt until well combined. Pour mixture into soufflé dish over caramelized sugar. Place dish in a large roasting pan with 3- to 4-inch-tall sides. (There should be least 1 inch space between the edge of the dish and the edge of the roasting pan.) Place roasting pan on oven rack. Pour enough hot water into roasting pan to come three-fourths of the way up the side of the roasting pan.

4. Bake about 1¼ hours or until a knife inserted in center comes out clean (custard will not appear set when gently shaken). Cool custard in roasting pan on a wire rack for 15 minutes. Remove dish from roasting pan and cool 2 hours on a wire rack. Cover with plastic wrap and chill overnight or up to 2 days.

5. Just before serving, run a thin metal spatula around edge of custard in dish. Place a rimmed serving plate slightly larger than the dish on top. Invert custard onto plate. In a skillet melt the 2 tablespoons butter; stir in cinnamon. Add banana slices. Cook for 4 minutes or until golden, turning once halfway through cooking. Arrange bananas on custard on serving plate. Spoon caramel sauce over the bananas.

Per serving: 296 cal., 11 g total fat (6 g sat. fat), 178 mg chol., 129 mg sodium, 44 g carbo., 0 g fiber, 7 g pro.

Banana Caramel Custard

Chocolate Flan

When you find an egg that is stuck to the carton, pouring a little water into the indentation and allowing it to stand for 5 minutes will release the egg.

Prep: 30 minutes **Bake:** 45 minutes
Stand: 10 minutes **Chill:** 6 hours **Oven:** 325°F
Makes: 12 servings

½ **cup sugar**
8 **ounces bittersweet chocolate, chopped**
4 **cups milk**
8 **eggs**
¾ **cup sugar**
½ **teaspoon ground cinnamon**

1. Preheat oven to 325°F. In a heavy 10-inch skillet cook the ½ cup sugar on medium-high heat until sugar begins to melt, shaking skillet occasionally to melt sugar evenly. Do not stir. When sugar starts to melt, reduce heat to low; cook about 5 minutes more or until all sugar is melted and golden brown, stirring with a wooden spoon. Immediately pour into a 9×2-inch round cake pan;* tilt to coat bottom. Let stand for 10 minutes.

2. In a heavy large saucepan heat and stir chocolate over low heat until melted. Gradually whisk in milk; heat and stir on medium until smooth. Remove saucepan from heat; set aside.

3. Meanwhile, in a bowl lightly beat eggs. Whisk the warm chocolate mixture, the ¾ cup sugar, and the cinnamon into eggs. Place cake pan in a large shallow roasting pan on oven rack. Pour chocolate mixture into cake pan. Pour boiling water into roasting pan around cake pan to a depth of 1 inch.

4. Bake for 45 to 50 minutes or until a knife inserted near the center comes out clean. Remove cake pan from water. Cool slightly on a wire rack. Cover and chill for 6 to 24 hours.

5. To unmold, loosen edge with knife, slipping point down side of pan to let in air. Invert a rimmed serving plate over pan; turn pan and plate over together. Remove pan.

***Note:** Use a 9×2-inch round cake pan. A pan with a 1½-inch side will not hold all of the egg mixture.

Per serving: 282 cal., 12 g total fat (6 g sat. fat) 148 mg chol., 80 mg sodium, 39 g carbo., 2 g fiber, 8 g pro.

Chocolate Flan

Chocolate-Orange Hazelnut Baklava

To thaw phyllo dough, allow it to stand overnight in the refrigerator.

Prep: 45 minutes **Bake:** 35 minutes **Oven:** 325°F
Makes: 24 to 48 baklava

- 3 **cups hazelnuts (filberts), toasted and inely chopped (see note, page 24)**
- 1⅓ **cups sugar**
- ¼ **cup unsweetened Dutch-process cocoa powder**
- ¾ **cup butter, melted**
- ½ **of a 16-ounce package frozen phyllo dough (14×9-inch rectangles), thawed**
- ¼ **cup water**
- ¼ **cup hazelnut syrup**
- 1 **teaspoon finely shredded orange peel**
- ¼ **cup orange juice**
  Unsweetened Dutch-process cocoa powder

1. Preheat oven to 325°F. For filling, in a large bowl stir together hazelnuts, ⅓ cup of the sugar, and the ¼ cup cocoa powder. Set aside.

2. Brush the bottom of a 13×9×2-inch baking pan with some of the melted butter. Unroll phyllo dough; cover with plastic wrap. (As you work, keep the phyllo covered to prevent it from drying out, removing sheets as you need them.) Layer one-fourth (5 or 6) of the phyllo sheets in the prepared baking pan, brushing each sheet generously with some of the melted butter. Sprinkle with about 1¼ cups of the filling. Repeat layering phyllo sheets and filling two more times, brushing each sheet with more butter.

3. Layer the remaining phyllo sheets on top of filling, brushing each sheet with more butter. Drizzle with any remaining butter. Using a sharp knife, cut into 24 to 48 diamond, rectangle, or square pieces.

4. Bake for 35 to 45 minutes or until golden brown. Cool slightly in pan on a wire rack.

Chocolate-Orange Hazelnut Baklava

5. Meanwhile, for syrup, in a medium saucepan stir together the remaining 1 cup sugar, the ¼ cup water, hazelnut syrup, orange peel, and orange juice. Bring to boiling; reduce heat. Simmer, uncovered, about 15 minutes or until reduced to 1 cup. Pour the syrup evenly over slightly cooled baklava in the pan. Cool completely. Before serving, sprinkle with additional cocoa powder.

Per baklava: 240 cal., 17 g total fat (5 g sat. fat), 15 mg chol., 87 mg sodium, 22 g carbo., 2 g fiber, 4 g pro.

baker's dozen

The tradition of baking Christmas cookies binds families together this time of year. Somehow these little rounds of sweetness—all sprinkled with holiday magic, rolled in love, and embellished with affection—have come to represent the greatest gifts of the season.

White Chocolate Candy Cane Drops

1. Preheat oven to 375°F. Line cookie sheet with parchment paper; set aside. Chop 4 ounces of the white chocolate; set aside. In a small saucepan cook and stir the remaining 4 ounces white chocolate on low heat until melted. Set aside to cool chocolate slightly.

2. In a large mixing bowl beat butter with an electric mixer on medium to high for 30 seconds. Add sugar, baking powder, and salt. Beat until combined, scraping sides of bowl occasionally. Beat in eggs and vanilla. Beat in melted white chocolate. Beat in as much of the flour as you can with the mixer. Stir in any remaining flour. Stir in the chopped white chocolate and crushed candy canes.

3. Drop dough by rounded teaspoons 2 inches apart onto prepared cookie sheet. Bake for 8 to 10 minutes or until cookies are lightly browned around edges. Transfer cookies to a wire rack and let cool.

Per cookie: 95 cal., 4 g total fat (2 g sat. fat), 14 mg chol., 52 mg sodium, 4 g carbo., 0 g fiber, 1 g pro.

White Chocolate Candy Cane Drops

To chop white chocolate, place chocolate squares on a cutting board, then using a heavy knife, shave off small bits.

Prep: 40 minutes **Bake:** 8 minutes per batch
Oven: 375°F **Makes:** about 50 cookies

- 8 ounces white chocolate baking squares with cocoa butter
- ½ cup butter, softened
- 1 cup sugar
- 1 teaspoon baking powder
- ½ teaspoon salt
- 2 eggs
- 1 teaspoon vanilla
- 2¾ cups all-purpose flour
- ⅔ cup finely crushed chocolate-filled peppermint candy canes or peppermint candy canes

Salty-Sweet Butterscotch Cookies

White whole wheat flour is ground from an albino variety of wheat. It provides a clever way to work whole grains into your baking—and no one will be able to detect the difference.

Prep: 35 minutes **Bake:** 8 minutes per batch
Oven: 375°F **Makes:** about 48 cookies

- ½ cup butter, softened
- 1 cup granulated sugar
- 1 cup packed brown sugar
- 1 teaspoon baking powder
- ½ teaspoon baking soda
- ½ teaspoon salt
- 2 eggs
- 2 teaspoons vanilla
- 2 cups white whole wheat flour or all-purpose flour
- ¾ cup coarsely chopped salted dry-roasted cashews
- ⅔ cup butterscotch-flavor pieces

1. Preheat oven to 375°F. In a large bowl beat butter with an electric mixer on medium to high for 30 seconds. Add granulated sugar, brown sugar, baking powder, baking soda, and salt. Beat until combined, scraping sides of bowl occasionally. Add eggs and vanilla; beat until combined. Beat in as much of the flour as you can with the mixer. Using a wooden spoon, stir in any remaining flour. Stir in cashews and butterscotch pieces.

2. Drop dough by rounded teaspoons 2 inches apart onto an ungreased cookie sheet. Bake for 8 to 10 minutes or until edges are lightly browned. Transfer cookies to a wire rack and let cool.

Per cookie: 101 cal., 4 g total fat (2 g sat. fat), 14 mg chol., 76 mg sodium, 15 g carbo., 0 g fiber, 1 g pro.

Macadamia Macaroons

Buttery-rich macadamia nuts—native to Australia— imbue macaroons with an irresistible crunchy texture.

Prep: 25 minutes Bake: 20 minutes per batch
Stand: 30 minutes Oven: 325°F
Makes: 26 cookies

2¾ **cups flaked coconut**
⅔ **cup sugar**
¼ **cup salted macadamia nuts, ground**
2 **tablespoons all-purpose flour**
¼ **teaspoon salt**
4 **egg whites, lightly beaten**
1 **teaspoon vanilla**
¾ **cup semisweet chocolate pieces**
2 **teaspoons shortening**
26 **salted macadamia nut pieces**

1. Preheat oven to 325°F. Line two large cookie sheets with parchment paper; set aside.

2. In a large bowl combine coconut, sugar, ground macadamia nuts, flour, and salt. Stir in egg whites and vanilla. Drop dough by rounded teaspoons 2 inches apart onto prepared cookie sheets. Using the teaspoons, make an indentation in each dough mound to create a "nest." Bake for 20 minutes or until browned. Transfer cookies to a wire rack; let cool.

3. In a saucepan combine chocolate pieces and shortening. Cook and stir on low heat until chocolate is melted and mixture is smooth. Spoon melted chocolate mixture into cookie centers. Place a macadamia nut piece on the chocolate center of each cookie. Let stand about 30 minutes or until chocolate is set.

Per cookie: 139 cal., 9 g total fat (5 g sat. fat), 0 mg chol., 75 mg sodium, 14 g carbo., 1 g fiber, 2 g pro.

Macadamia Macaroons

Pistachio-Lime Balls

To make these zesty morsels ahead of time, shape into balls, roll in colored sugar, place in a single layer on a baking sheet, cover tightly, and freeze. Thaw cookies for 10 minutes before baking.

Prep: 25 minutes **Bake:** 15 minutes per batch
Cool: 5 minutes per batch **Oven:** 325°F
Makes: about 48 cookies

- 1 **cup butter, softened**
- ½ **cup powdered sugar**
- 2 **cups all-purpose flour**
- 1 **cup coarsely ground dry-roasted pistachio nuts**
- 1 **tablespoon finely shredded lime peel**
  Green and/or yellow fine or coarse colored sugar
  Powdered sugar

1. Preheat oven to 325°F. Beat butter in a large mixing bowl with an electric mixer on medium to high for 30 seconds. Beat in ½ cup powdered sugar until combined, scraping sides of bowl occasionally. Beat in as much flour as you can with the mixer. Stir in any remaining flour, the pistachio nuts, and lime peel with a wooden spoon.

2. Shape dough into 1-inch balls. Roll each ball in green sugar. Place balls 2 inches apart on ungreased cookie sheets. Bake for 15 minutes or until bottoms are lightly brown. Cool 5 minutes on cookie sheets on wire racks. Sprinkle warm cookies with powdered sugar. Transfer cookies to wire racks and cool completely.

3. If desired, roll cooled cookies in additional powdered sugar or colored sugars before serving.

Per cookie: 79 cal., 5 g total fat (3 g sat. fat), 10 mg chol., 28 mg sodium, 7 g carbo., 0 g fiber, 1 g pro.

Pistachio-Lime Balls

Cappuccino Love Bites

These delightfully dainty cookies will make your kitchen smell like your favorite coffeehouse.

Prep: 25 minutes **Chill:** 1 hour
Bake: 10 minutes per batch **Oven:** 350°F
Makes: 48 cookies

- 1 **cup butter-flavor shortening**
- 1½ **cups sugar**
- 1 **teaspoon baking powder**
- ¼ **teaspoon salt**
- 1 **egg**
- 1 **tablespoon coffee-flavor liqueur or milk**
- 1 **teaspoon vanilla**
- 2¼ **cups all-purpose flour**
- 2 **tablespoons instant coffee crystals**
- 48 **milk chocolate kisses with stripes**

1. In a large bowl beat shortening with an electric mixer on medium to high for 30 seconds. Add 1 cup of the sugar, baking powder, and salt. Beat until mixture is combined, scraping sides of bowl occasionally. Beat in egg, liqueur, and vanilla until combined. Beat in as much flour as you can with the mixer. Stir in any remaining flour. If necessary, cover and chill dough in the refrigerator about 1 hour or until easy to handle.

2. Preheat oven to 350°F. Lightly grease cookie sheets; set aside. Shape dough into 1-inch balls. Combine remaining ½ cup sugar and coffee crystals. Roll dough balls in sugar mixture. Place balls 2 inches apart on prepared cookie sheets.

3. Bake for 10 minutes or until tops are cracked and sides are set; do not let edges brown. Immediately press a chocolate kiss into the center of each cookie. If desired, while chocolate is still warm, swirl it gently with your finger or a knife. Transfer cookies to wire racks and cool completely.

Per cookie: 111 cal., 6 g total fat (2 g sat. fat), 6 mg chol., 25 mg sodium, 13 g carbo., 0 g fiber, 1 g pro.

1. Preheat oven to 325°F. In a large bowl beat butter with an electric mixer on medium to high for 30 seconds. Add the 1½ cups granulated sugar, the baking soda, cream of tartar, and salt. Beat until well mixed. Add oil, egg, vanilla, and lemon extract. Beat until well mixed. Beat in as much of the flour as you can with the mixer. Using a wooden spoon, stir in any remaining flour and the lemon peel.

2. Shape dough into ¾-inch balls. Place balls 2 inches apart on an ungreased cookie sheet. Dip the bottom of a glass in additional granulated sugar and slightly flatten each cookie.

3. Bake for 10 minutes or just until edges start to brown. Transfer to a wire rack and let cool.

4. Spread about ½ teaspoon of the lemon curd on the bottom of each of half of the cookies. Top with remaining cookies, flat sides down, pressing lightly together. If desired, sprinkle tops of assembled sandwich cookies with powdered sugar and colored sugar.

Per sandwich cookie: 110 cal., 5 g total fat (2 g sat. fat), 12 mg chol., 62 mg sodium, 15 g carbo., 1 g fiber, 1 g pro.

Zesty Lemon Tea Sandwiches

Light and lovely lemon cookies add interest and diversity to holiday cookie trays.

Prep: 45 minutes **Bake:** 10 minutes per batch
Oven: 325°F **Makes:** about 60 sandwich cookies

¾	**cup butter, softened**
1½	**cups granulated sugar**
1½	**teaspoons baking soda**
1½	**teaspoons cream of tartar**
¼	**teaspoon salt**
¾	**cup cooking oil**
1	**egg**
1	**teaspoon vanilla**
1	**teaspoon lemon extract**
4	**cups all-purpose flour**
1½	**teaspoons finely shredded lemon peel**
	Granulated sugar
⅔	**cup purchased lemon curd**
	Powdered sugar (optional)
	Colored sugar (optional)

Zesty Lemon Tea Sandwiches

Vanilla Bean Angel Pillows

Vanilla Bean Angel Pillows

Cornstarch is the surprise ingredient in these incredibly light butter cookies—it gives these heavenly bites a celestial texture that melts in your mouth.

Prep: 30 minutes **Bake:** 12 minutes per batch
Cool: 5 minutes **Oven:** 350°F
Makes: about 28 cookies

1½ **cups all-purpose flour**
½ **cup powdered sugar**
¼ **cup cornstarch**
¼ **teaspoon salt**
1 **vanilla bean, split in half lengthwise**
1 **cup cold butter, cubed**
¼ **cup vanilla sugar***

1. Preheat oven to 350°F. In a food processor combine flour, powdered sugar, cornstarch, and salt. Cover and process until combined.

2. Using the tip of a sharp knife, scrape pulp from vanilla bean. Add vanilla pulp to the flour mixture; add butter. Cover and process with several on/off pulses until mixture starts to cling, stopping once to scrape down sides of bowl. Gather mixture into a ball.

3. Shape dough into 1¼-inch balls. Place 2 inches apart on an ungreased cookie sheet.

4. Bake for 12 minutes or just until edges start to brown. Transfer cookies to a wire rack; cool for 5 minutes.

5. Place vanilla sugar in a small bowl. While still warm, roll cookies in vanilla sugar to coat. Cool completely on wire rack.

***Note:** To make vanilla sugar, in a small bowl combine 1 cup sugar and 1 vanilla bean, split in half lengthwise. Cover and let stand at room temperature for 1 week.

Per cookie: 103 cal., 7 g total fat (4 g sat. fat), 17 mg chol., 68 mg sodium, 10 g carbo., 0 g fiber, 1 g pro.

White Christmas Crinkles

For the most exquisite white chocolate flavor, choose white chocolate with creamy white—rather than stark white—color. Swiss brands are especially good.

Prep: 50 minutes **Chill:** 2 hours
Bake: 8 minutes per batch **Oven:** 375°F
Makes: about 42 cookies

8	ounces white chocolate baking squares (with cocoa butter)
2	cups all-purpose flour
½	teaspoon baking soda
¼	teaspoon salt
⅓	cup butter, softened
1	cup sugar
1	egg
¼	cup buttermilk or sour milk*
1	teaspoon vanilla
	Sugar
1	tablespoon shortening

1. Coarsely chop 4 ounces of the white chocolate. In a small saucepan cook and stir chopped white chocolate over low heat until melted and smooth. Set aside. In a small bowl stir together flour, baking soda, and salt. Set aside.

2. In a large bowl beat butter with an electric mixer on medium to high for 30 seconds. Add the 1 cup sugar. Beat until combined, scraping sides of bowl occasionally. Beat in melted white chocolate, egg, buttermilk, and vanilla. Beat in flour mixture until combined. Cover and chill about 2 hours or until dough is easy to handle.

3. Preheat oven to 375°F. Place additional sugar in a bowl. Shape dough into 1-inch balls; roll in sugar to coat. Place balls 2 inches apart on an ungreased cookie sheet. Bake for 8 to 10 minutes or until tops are lightly browned. Cool on cookie sheet for 1 minute. Transfer cookies to a wire rack; let cool.

4. In a small saucepan cook and stir the remaining 4 ounces white chocolate and the shortening on low heat until melted and smooth. Spoon melted chocolate into a small resealable plastic bag. Seal bag; snip off a small corner of the bag. Pipe melted chocolate in a spiral design on each cookie. Let stand until chocolate is set.

*Note: To make ¼ cup sour milk, place ¾ teaspoon lemon juice or vinegar in a glass measuring cup. Add enough milk to equal ¼ cup total liquid; stir. Let mixture stand for 5 minutes before using.

Per cookie: 94 cal., 4 g total fat (2 g sat. fat), 10 mg chol., 48 mg sodium, 14 g carbo., 0 g fiber, 1 g pro.

Tropical Cookies

These super-imple cookies bring breezy thoughts of hot sun and sandy beaches to cold northern winters.

Prep: 20 minutes **Bake:** 11 minutes per batch
Oven: 375°F **Makes:** 24 cookies

1½	cups flaked coconut
2	tablespoons milk
1	18-ounce package refrigerated ready-to-bake white chocolate and macadamia nut cookie dough (12 cookies)
2	ounces white baking chocolate (with cocoa butter)
½	teaspoon shortening

1. Preheat oven to 375°F. Line two cookie sheets with parchment paper or foil; set aside. Place coconut in a shallow dish. Place milk in a small bowl. Divide each cookie dough piece in half. Using your hands, roll each dough piece into a ball. Roll each ball in milk, then in coconut to coat. Place balls 2 inches apart on prepared cookie sheets.

2. Bake for 11 to 13 minutes or until set and coconut browns. Remove from oven. Cool on cookie sheet for 1 minute. Transfer cookies to a wire rack and cool.

3. In a small saucepan combine white baking chocolate and shortening; cook and stir over low heat until melted. Drizzle each cookie with some of the melted mixture. If necessary, chill cookies about 15 minutes to firm chocolate.

Per cookie: 149 cal., 9 g total fat (5 g sat. fat), 5 mg chol., 77 mg sodium, 16 g carbo., 1 g fiber, 2 g pro.

Bittersweet Chocolate and Peppermint Sandwiches

If dough becomes soft, sticky, or at all troublesome while cutting strips, simply return it to the refrigerator for a few minutes.

Prep: 1 hour **Chill:** 1 hour
Bake: 7 minutes per batch
Oven: 350°F **Makes:** about 36 sandwich cookies

- ¾ cup butter, softened
- 1 cup granulated sugar
- ½ teaspoon baking powder
- 1 egg
- 2 cups all-purpose flour
- ¼ cup butter, softened
- 2 cups powdered sugar
- 1 to 2 tablespoons milk
- ½ teaspoon peppermint extract
  Pink food coloring (optional)
- 3 ounces dark or bittersweet chocolate, melted and slightly cooled

1. In a large bowl beat the ¾ cup butter with an electric mixer on medium to high for 30 seconds. Add granulated sugar and baking powder; beat until combined. Beat in egg. Beat in as much of the flour as you can with the mixer. Using a wooden spoon, stir in any remaining flour.

2. Divide dough in half. Place each dough half between two sheets of waxed paper; roll each to a 12×10-inch rectangle. Chill dough rectangles for 30 minutes.

3. Preheat oven to 350°F. Remove top sheets of waxed paper. Using a fluted pastry wheel or pizza cutter, cut each dough rectangle lengthwise into 10 strips and crosswise into 6 strips to make sixty 2×1-inch rectangles per dough half (120 rectangles total). Transfer dough rectangles to an ungreased cookie sheet, leaving 1 inch between rectangles. (If necessary, chill dough about 15 minutes more before transferring.) Bake for 7 to 9 minutes or until edges are very lightly browned. Transfer cookies to a wire rack and let cool.

4. For frosting, in a medium bowl beat the ¼ cup butter on medium to high for 30 seconds. Add 1 cup of the powdered sugar, 1 tablespoon of the milk, and peppermint extract; beat until smooth. Beat in the remaining 1 cup powdered sugar and enough of the remaining milk to make a frosting of spreading consistency. If desired, use food coloring to tint frosting pink.

5. To assemble, pipe or spread a little of the frosting on the bottom of one cookie; top with a second cookie, flat side down, and press lightly together. Pipe or spread with more of the frosting; top with a third cookie, flat side down. Repeat with

the remaining cookies and the remaining frosting. Pipe dots of melted chocolate around edges of each assembled sandwich cookie or drizzle the melted chocolate over cookies.* Chill about 30 minutes or until chocolate is set.

*Note: To decorate the assembled sandwich cookies with chocolate, fill a heavy-duty resealable plastic bag with the melted chocolate and snip a small hole in one corner of the bag. Squeeze the bag, piping the chocolate over the cookies in dots or drizzles.

Per sandwich cookie: 133 cal., 6 g total fat (14 g sat. fat), 20 mg chol., 44 mg sodium, 19 g carbo., 0 g fiber, 1 g pro.

Two-Tone Peanut Butter Slices

For the best results, use regular peanut butter for this recipe. The behavior of peanut butters labeled "natural" can be unpredictable in baked goods.

Prep: 40 minutes **Chill:** 2 hours
Bake: 8 minutes per batch
Oven: 375°F **Makes:** about 120 cookies

¾	cup creamy peanut butter
½	cup butter, softened
½	cup granulated sugar
½	cup packed brown sugar
½	teaspoon baking powder
½	teaspoon baking soda
1	egg
1	teaspoon vanilla
1½	cups all-purpose flour
1½	ounces unsweetened chocolate, melted and slightly cooled

1. In a bowl beat peanut butter and butter with an electric mixer on medium to high for 30 seconds. Add granulated sugar, brown sugar, baking powder, and baking soda. Beat until combined, scraping sides of bowl occasionally. Beat in egg and vanilla. Beat in as much of the flour as you can with the mixer. Stir in any remaining flour.

2. Divide dough in half. Stir melted chocolate into one portion of dough. Divide each dough portion in half. On a lightly floured surface, roll each portion

Two-Tone Peanut Butter Slices

of dough into a 10-inch-long log. Wrap and chill logs for 1 to 2 hours or until firm.

3. Cut logs in half lengthwise. Place cut side of one peanut butter log and cut side of one chocolate log together; press to seal. Roll the log lightly to smooth seams. Repeat with remaining log halves. Wrap and chill logs for 1 hour or until firm.

4. Preheat oven to 375°F. Cut logs into ¼-inch-thick slices. Place slices 1 inch apart on ungreased cookie sheet. Bake cookies for 8 minutes or until edges are lightly browned and slightly firm. Transfer cookies to a wire rack and let cool.

Per cookie: 31 cal., 2 g total fat (1 g sat. fat), 4 mg chol., 21 mg sodium, 3 g carbo., 0 g fiber, 1 g pro.

Sugar and Spice Coffee Slices

Sugar and Spice Coffee Slices

These crisp cookies are destined for dipping. Enjoy them with coffee, tea, or hot cocoa.

Prep: 25 minutes **Chill:** 2 hours
Bake: 9 minutes per batch **Oven:** 375°F
Makes: about 4 dozen cookies

½ **cup butter, softened**
¼ **cup shortening**
1 **cup granulated sugar**
½ **cup packed brown sugar**
1 **teaspoon baking powder**
1 **teaspoon ground cinnamon**
¼ **teaspoon salt**
2 **tablespoons instant espresso powder**
1 **tablespoon hot water**
1 **egg**
2 **cups all-purpose flour**
1 **recipe Coffee Topping**
   Coffee beans (optional)

1. In a large mixing bowl beat butter and shortening with an electric mixer on medium to high for 30 seconds. Add granulated sugar, brown sugar, baking powder, cinnamon, and salt. Beat until combined, scraping sides of bowl occasionally. In a small bowl stir together the espresso powder and hot water until dissolved. Add to sugar mixture along with the egg; beat until combined. Beat in as much of the flour as you can with the mixer. Using a wooden spoon, stir in any remaining flour.

2. Divide dough into thirds. Shape each portion into a 7×2×1-inch loaf. Wrap each loaf in plastic wrap; chill dough about 2 hours or until firm.

3. Preheat oven to 375°F. Cut loaves into ⅜-inch-thick slices. Place slices about 2 inches apart on an ungreased cookie sheet. Sprinkle slices with Coffee Topping. If desired, gently press a few coffee beans onto each slice.

4. Bake for 9 to 10 minutes or until edges are light brown. Let stand for 1 minute on cookie sheet. Transfer to a wire rack and let cool.

Coffee Topping: In a small bowl stir together ¼ cup granulated sugar and 1 teaspoon instant espresso powder.

Per cookie: 77 cal., 3 g total fat (2 g sat. fat), 9 mg chol., 37 mg sodium, 12 g carbo., 0 g fiber, 0 g pro.

Red Velvet Whoopie Pies with Peppermint Filling

Whoopie Pies are the hottest trend to hit baking since the cupcake craze. With their festive color and wintery taste, these will become a Christmastime favorite.

Prep: 45 minutes Bake: 7 minutes per batch
Oven: 375°F Makes: about 40 whoopie pies

- ½ **cup butter, softened**
- 1 **cup packed brown sugar**
- 2 **tablespoons unsweetened cocoa powder**
- ½ **teaspoon baking soda**
- ¼ **teaspoon salt**
- 1 **egg**
- 1 **teaspoon vanilla**
- 2 **cups all-purpose flour**
- ½ **cup buttermilk**
- 1 **1-ounce bottle red food coloring (2 tablespoons)**
- 1 **recipe Peppermint and Cream Cheese Filling**
  Striped round peppermint candies, finely chopped (optional)

1. Preheat oven to 375°F. Line a cookie sheet with parchment paper; set aside. In a large bowl beat the ½ cup butter with an electric mixer on medium to high for 30 seconds. Add the brown sugar, cocoa powder, baking soda, and salt. Beat until combined, scraping bowl occasionally. Beat in egg and vanilla until combined. Alternately add flour and buttermilk, beating on low after each addition just until mixtures are combined. Stir in red food coloring.

2. Place rounded teaspoons of dough 2 inches apart onto prepared cookie sheet. Bake for 7 to 9 minutes or until edges are set. Cool on cookie sheet for 2 minutes. Transfer cookies to a wire rack; let cool.

3. Spread Peppermint and Cream Cheese Filling on bottom of each of half of the cookies. Top with remaining cookies, flat sides down, pressing lightly together. If desired, sprinkle each filled cookie with chopped peppermint candies.

4. Serve cookies immediately. If chilled, let stand at room temperature for 15 minutes before serving.

Peppermint and Cream Cheese Filling: In a large bowl combine two 3-ounce packages cream cheese, softened; 3 tablespoons butter, softened; and ½ teaspoon peppermint extract. Beat with an electric mixer on medium until light and fluffy. Gradually beat in 3 cups powdered sugar. If necessary, add milk (1 teaspoon at a time) to make a filling of spreading consistency.

Per whoopie pie: 128 cal., 5 g total fat (3 g sat. fat), 18 mg chol., 73 mg sodium, 20 g carbo., 0 g fiber, 1 g pro.

Red Velvet Whoopie Pies with Peppermint Filling

Cashew Torte Cookies

The cashew-lovers in your clan will adore you for treating them to these rounds of nutty goodness.

Prep: 50 minutes **Chill:** 4 hours
Bake: 8 minutes per batch **Oven:** 375°F
Stand: 30 minutes **Makes:** about 28 cookies

- ½ **cup shortening**
- ½ **cup butter, softened**
- 1 **cup granulated sugar**
- ¼ **cup packed brown sugar**
- ½ **teaspoon baking soda**
- ¼ **teaspoon baking powder**
- ¼ **teaspoon salt**
- 2 **eggs**
- 1 **teaspoon vanilla**
- 2½ **cups all-purpose flour**
- ¾ **cup lightly salted cashews, ground**
  Cashew halves
- 1 **8-ounce container mascarpone cheese or one 8-ounce package cream cheese, softened**
- ¼ **cup apple butter**
- 2 **tablespoons packed brown sugar**
- ¼ **teaspoon ground mace or ground nutmeg**
  Sifted powdered sugar (optional)
  Ground mace or ground nutmeg (optional)

1. In a large mixing bowl beat shortening and butter with an electric mixer on medium to high for 30 seconds. Add granulated sugar, the ¼ cup brown sugar, baking soda, baking powder, and salt and beat until combined, scraping sides of bowl occasionally. Add eggs and vanilla and beat until combined. Beat in as much of the flour as you can with the mixer. Stir in any remaining flour and the ground nuts with a wooden spoon.

2. Divide the dough into 4 equal portions. Shape each portion into a 6-inch-long roll. Wrap rolls in plastic wrap or waxed paper. Chill for 4 to 24 hours or until firm.

3. Preheat oven to 375°F. Cut rolls into ¼-inch slices. Place slices 1 inch apart on an ungreased cookie sheet. Press cashew halves into the tops of 28 of the cookies. Bake for 8 minutes or until edges are firm and lightly golden. Transfer cookies to a wire rack to cool.

4. Meanwhile, for filling, in a bowl stir together mascarpone, apple butter, the 2 tablespoons brown sugar, and mace until smooth. About 30 minutes before serving, spread about 1 teaspoon filling on a plain cookie; top with a second plain cookie. Spread about 1 teaspoon filling on the second cookie. Top with a nut-topped cookie. Repeat with remaining cookies and filling. If desired, sprinkle tops with sifted powdered sugar and additional ground mace. Let stacked cookies stand about 30 minutes before serving to soften.

Per cookie: 223 cal., 13 g total fat (6 g sat. fat), 34 mg chol., 91 mg sodium, 24 g carbo., 1 g fiber, 4 g pro.

Lemon-Cardamom Meringue Cookies

Cardamom's warm, sweet spiciness radiates from these featherlight cookies.

Prep: 35 minutes **Bake:** 20 minutes
Stand: 30 minutes **Oven:** 300°F **Makes:** 30 cookies

- 3 **egg whites**
- ¼ **cup sugar**
- 1 **tablespoon cornstarch**
- ⅛ **teaspoon ground cardamom**

½ teaspoon vanilla
¼ teaspoon cream of tartar
1 teaspoon finely shredded lemon, lime, or orange peel

1. Let egg whites stand at room temperature for 30 minutes. Line a very large cookie sheet (or 2 smaller cookie sheets) with parchment paper or foil; set aside. In a small bowl stir together sugar, cornstarch, and cardamom; set aside.

2. Preheat oven to 300°F. In a medium bowl combine egg whites, vanilla, and cream of tartar. Beat with an electric mixer on high until soft peaks form (tips curl). Gradually add the sugar mixture, 1 tablespoon at a time, beating on high until stiff peaks form (tips stand straight). Fold in citrus peel.

3. Spoon egg white mixture into a piping bag fitted with an extra-large star tip. Pipe mixture into 30 swirls onto prepared cookie sheet, making each swirl about 2 inches in diameter and 1½ inches tall and leaving a 1½-inch space between swirls. (Or spoon egg white mixture into a resealable plastic bag. Snip off one corner. Pipe into 30 "kiss" shapes that are the same size as the swirls.)

4. Bake for 20 minutes. Turn off oven. Let cookies dry in oven, with door closed, for 30 minutes. Remove from oven and gently peel off the parchment paper or foil.

Per cookie: 9 cal., 0 g total fat, 0 mg chol., 6 mg sodium, 2 g carbo., 0 g fiber, 0 g pro.

Raspberry Shortbread Logs

When baking shortbread, be sure to use real butter. Whipped butter products, with air incorporated, may adversely affect baking recipes.

Prep: 20 minutes **Bake:** 30 minutes **Oven:** 325°F
Makes: about 14 cookies

1¼ cups all-purpose flour
3 tablespoons packed brown sugar
½ cup cold butter
¼ cup pecans, finely chopped
4 teaspoons seedless raspberry jam

or apricot preserves
½ cup powdered sugar
1 tablespoon rum, brandy, or milk

1. Preheat oven to 325°F. In a large bowl combine flour and brown sugar. Using a pastry blender, cut in the butter until mixture resembles fine crumbs. Stir in pecans. Knead mixture until it forms a ball.

2. Divide dough in half. On a lightly floured surface, roll each portion of dough into a 7-inch-long log. Place logs 4 inches apart on ungreased cookie sheet. Using a fingertip, make a ¼-inch-deep groove down the center of each log, leaving a ½-inch edge on the ends. Stir jam until nearly smooth (snip any large pieces of fruit if using apricot preserves). Spoon jam into grooves.

3. Bake for 30 minutes or until logs are lightly browned. Cool logs completely on cookie sheet on wire rack. Cut each log into 1-inch slices.

4. In a small bowl combine powdered sugar and rum; stir until smooth. Drizzle over cookie slices.

Per cookie: 148 cal., 8 g total fat (4 g sat. fat), 17 mg chol., 48 mg sodium, 17 g carbo., 1 g fiber, 1 g pro.

Raspberry Shortbread Logs

Almond Apricot Windows

As breathtaking as stained-glass windows, these sandwich cookies may just be the prettiest ones on your cookie platter.

Prep: 50 minutes **Chill:** 2 hours
Bake: 10 minutes per batch **Oven:** 325°F
Makes: about 30 sandwich cookies

1	cup blanched almonds, toasted and chopped
1	tablespoon sugar
1	cup butter, softened
⅔	cup sugar
1	egg
1	egg yolk
½	teaspoon salt
½	teaspoon vanilla
½	teaspoon almond extract
¼	teaspoon ground nutmeg
2⅔	cups all-purpose flour
¾	cup apricot jam
	Powdered sugar (optional)

1. In a food processor combine almonds and the 1 tablespoon sugar. Cover and process until nuts are finely ground. Set aside.

2. In a bowl beat butter with an electric mixer on medium for 30 seconds. Add the ⅔ cup sugar. Beat until combined. Add the finely ground almonds, the egg, egg yolk, salt, vanilla, almond extract, and nutmeg, beating until combined. Beat in flour until combined. Divide dough into 4 portions. Cover and chill 2 hours or until dough is easy to handle.

3. Preheat oven to 325°F. Between waxed paper, roll out one of the dough portion to about a ¼-inch thickness. Peel off top sheet of paper. Using a fluted 2-inch cookie cutter, cut out dough. Place dough cutouts 1 inch apart on an ungreased cookie sheet. Using a fluted 1-inch cookie cutter, cut out centers from half of the dough cutouts.

4. Bake for 10 to 12 minutes or until tops are a pale golden brown. Cool on cookie sheet for 2 minutes. Transfer cookies to a wire rack and let cool. Repeat with the remaining dough portions.

5. Spread 1 slightly rounded teaspoon of the jam into the center of each whole cookie. Top with the cutout cookies, flat sides down, pressing lightly together. If desired, dust tops of cookies with powdered sugar.

Per cookie: 169 cal., 9 g total fat (4 g sat. fat), 30 mg chol., 89 mg sodium, 20 g carbo., 1 g fiber, 3 g pro.

Almond Apricot Windows

Maple Pecan Shortbread

Maple and pecans grace this buttery shortbread with autumnal flavors.

Prep: 20 minutes **Bake:** 25 minutes per batch
Oven: 325°F **Makes:** 24 wedges

1	cup butter, softened
½	cup granulated sugar
1	teaspoon vanilla
1	teaspoon maple flavoring
1	teaspoon finely shredded orange peel
2	cups all-purpose flour
½	cup pecans, toasted and finely chopped
	Coarse sugar

1. Preheat oven to 325°F. In a large bowl beat butter with an electric mixer on medium to high for 30 seconds. Add granulated sugar. Beat until mixture is fluffy and light in color, scraping sides of bowl occasionally. Beat in vanilla, maple flavoring, and orange peel until combined. Beat in as much of the flour as you can with the mixer. Using a wooden spoon, stir in any remaining flour and the pecans.

2. Divide dough in half. Press one portion of the dough evenly into the bottom of an 8-inch fluted tart pan that has a removable bottom. (Wrap the remaining dough with plastic wrap and set aside.) Sprinkle with coarse sugar. Prick every inch or so with the tines of a fork. Cut into 12 wedges, leaving the dough in the pan.

3. Bake for 25 to 27 minutes or until top is pale golden brown. Cut into wedges again while warm. Cool in pan on a wire rack for 5 minutes. Remove wedges from pan and cool completely on wire rack. Wash the tart pan and repeat with the remaining dough.

Per wedge: 141 cal., 9 g total fat (5 g sat. fat), 20 mg chol., 55 mg sodium, 13 g carbo., 0 g fiber, 1 g pro.

Madeleines with Vanilla Bean Buttercream

Madeleines with Vanilla Bean Buttercream

Madeleine [MAD-l-ihn] molds can be purchased at specialty bakeware stores or on the Internet.

Prep: 30 minutes **Bake:** 10 minutes per batch
Oven: 375°F **Makes:** 48 cookies

- 4 **eggs**
- 1 **teaspoon vanilla**
- 2 **cups powdered sugar**
- 1⅓ **cups all-purpose flour**
- ½ **teaspoon baking powder**
- 1 **cup butter, melted and cooled**
- 1 **recipe Vanilla Bean Buttercream**

1. Preheat oven to 375°F. Grease and flour forty-eight 3-inch madeleine molds; set aside.

2. In a large bowl combine eggs and vanilla. Beat with an electric mixer on high for 4 minutes.

Gradually beat in the 2 cups powdered sugar, scraping sides of bowl occasionally. Beat about 5 minutes more or until thick and satiny.

3. In a small bowl stir together flour and baking powder. Sift about one-fourth of the flour mixture over egg mixture; stir in gently. Repeat, stirring in remaining flour mixture by fourths. Stir in melted butter. Spoon batter into prepared molds, filling each mold about three-fourths full.

4. Bake for 10 to 12 minutes or until edges are golden and tops spring back when lightly touched. Cool in molds on wire racks for 1 minute. Using a knife, loosen edges of madelines from molds. Invert onto wire racks and let cool. To serve, spread madelines with Vanilla Bean Buttercream.

Vanilla Bean Buttercream: In a large bowl beat ½ cup softened butter with an electric mixer on medium to high for 30 seconds. Using one-fourth of a vanilla bean that has been split in half lengthwise, scrape pulp from bean with the tip of a sharp knife. Add vanilla pulp to butter; beat until combined. Gradually beat in 3 cups powdered sugar until combined. Beat in enough milk (3 to 4 tablespoons total) to make frosting of spreading consistency.

Per madeline: 89 cal., 6 g total fat (4 g sat. fat), 33 mg chol., 51 mg sodium, 8 g carbo., 0 g fiber, 1 g pro.

Cherry Cheesecake Bars

smooth. Beat in reserved cherry liquid until combined. Stir in egg whites and chopped cherries.

5. Pour cream cheese mixture over partially baked crust, spreading evenly. Bake for 20 to 25 minutes or until set. Cool in pan on a wire rack for 1 hour. Cover and refrigerate for 4 to 24 hours. Cut into bars.

Per bar: 157 cal., 9 g total fat (5 g sat. fat), 21 mg chol., 96 mg sodium, 18 g carbo., 0 g fiber, 2 g pro.

Cherry Cheesecake Bars

Maraschino cherries—fresh cherries macerated in sugar syrup—are most often made using Queen Anne cherries.

Prep: 25 minutes **Bake:** 30 minutes **Cool:** 1 hour
Chill: 4 hours **Oven:** 350°F **Makes:** 32 bars

- 2   **cups finely crushed vanilla wafers (about 55 wafers)**
- ⅓   **cup butter, melted**
- 1   **10-ounce jar maraschino cherries**
- 2   **8-ounce packages cream cheese, softened**
- 1   **cup sugar**
- 5   **egg whites, slightly beaten**

1. Preheat oven to 350°F. Line a 13×9×2-inch baking pan with foil, extending foil over edges of pan; set baking pan aside.

2. For crust, stir together crushed cookies and melted butter in a medium bowl. Press mixture evenly on bottom of prepared pan. Bake for 10 minutes.

3. Meanwhile, drain cherries well, reserving 2 tablespoons of the cherry liquid. If necessary, remove and discard stems from cherries. Finely chop the cherries; set cherries aside.

4. Beat cream cheese and sugar in a large mixing bowl with an electric mixer on medium until

Peanutty Buckeye Bars

Buckeye cookies are peanut butter balls dipped in chocolate. With this quick-and-easy bar recipe, you get the same enticing taste with less work.

Prep: 20 minutes **Bake:** 25 minutes **Oven:** 350°F
Makes: 32 bars

- 1   **19.5-ounce package brownie mix**
- 2   **eggs**
- ⅓   **cup cooking oil**
- 1   **cup chopped peanuts**
- 1   **14-ounce can sweetened condensed milk**
- ½   **cup peanut butter**

1. Preheat oven to 350°F. Lightly grease a 13×9×2-inch baking pan; set aside. In a large bowl combine brownie mix, eggs, and oil. Beat with an electric mixer on medium until combined. Stir in peanuts. Remove half of the brownie mixture and set aside. Spread the remaining brownie mixture evenly into prepared pan.

2. In a medium bowl whisk together sweetened condensed milk and peanut butter until smooth. Spread evenly over brownie mixture in pan. Separate the remaining brownie mixture into pieces, flatten them with your fingers, and place them on top of the brownie mixture in pan.

3. Bake for 25 to 30 minutes or until top is set and edges are lightly browned. Cool completely in pan on a wire rack. Cut into bars.

Per bar: 184 cal., 9 g total fat (2 g sat. fat), 17 mg chol., 118 mg sodium, 23 g carbo., 1 g fiber, 4 g pro.

Raspberry and White Chocolate Brownies

Another time, make these not-at-all-brown brownies with blackberries—the results will be equally superb.

Prep: 30 minutes **Bake:** 30 minutes
Oven: 350°F **Makes:** 20 brownies

- ½ cup butter
- 2 ounces white baking chocolate, chopped
- 2 eggs
- ⅔ cup sugar
- 1 teaspoon vanilla
- 1 cup all-purpose flour
- ½ cup chopped toasted almonds
- ½ teaspoon baking powder
  Dash salt
- 1 cup fresh raspberries
- 2 ounces white baking chocolate, melted

1. Preheat oven to 350°F. Line an 8×8×2-inch baking pan with foil, about 1 inch of foil extending over the edges of pan. Grease foil; set aside.

2. In a medium saucepan heat and stir butter and the chopped white chocolate on low heat until smooth. Remove from heat. Add eggs, sugar, and vanilla. Beat lightly with a wooden spoon just until combined. Stir in the flour, almonds, baking powder, and salt. Spread batter evenly in the prepared pan. Sprinkle with raspberries.

3. Bake for 30 to 35 minutes or until golden. Cool in pan on a wire rack. Remove brownies from pan, using the foil to lift brownies. Place on cutting board; cut into bars. Drizzle bars with the melted white chocolate. Serve brownies the same day they are prepared.

Per brownie: 146 cal., 8 g total fat (4 g sat. fat), 34 mg chol., 62 mg sodium, 16 g carbo., 1 g fiber, 2 g pro.

Raspberry and White Chocolate Brownies

candies and confections

When sugarplums start dancing in your head,
kick up your heels and join right in. Whip up
any one of these luscious homemade
candies—whether chocolaty, nutty, or filled
with fruits, each one of these goodies will hit
the dance floor in style.

Peanutty Brittle, page 121

Tropical Candy Drops

Tropical-blend dried fruits most often contain pineapple, mang,o and papaya—all of which have a special affinity for white chocolate.

Prep: 10 minutes **Cook:** 8 minutes
Chill: 30 minutes **Makes:** about 35 candy drops

    8 ounces vanilla-flavor candy coating or
       white chocolate baking squares (with
       cocoa butter), coarsely chopped
    1 tablespoon shortening
    1 cup tropical-blend mixed dried fruit bits
    ¾ cup macadamia nuts, coarsely chopped
    ¾ cup shredded coconut, toasted*

1. Line a cookie sheet with waxed paper; set aside.

2. In a heavy medium saucepan combine candy coating and 1 tablespoon shortening. Cook and stir mixture on low heat for 8 to 10 minutes or until candy coating or white chocolate is melted.

Remove from heat. Add dried fruit, nuts, and coconut. Quickly drop mixture by teaspoonfuls about 1 inch apart onto the waxed paper.

3. Chill candies on cookie sheet about 30 minutes or until set. Store candies in an airtight container for up to 1 week at room temperature, 2 weeks in the refrigerator, or 3 months in the freezer.

*Note: To toast coconut, preheat oven to 350°F. Spread coconut in a single layer in a baking pan. Bake for 5 to 10 minutes or until coconut is light golden color, watching carefully and stirring once or twice so coconut does not burn.

Per candy drop: 82 cal., 5 g total fat (3 g sat. fat), 0 mg chol., 14 mg sodium, 9 g carbo., 1 g fiber, 0 g pro.

Tropical Holiday Triangles

If your raisins seem too dry, place them in a microwavable dish, add 2 teaspoons water, cover with plastic wrap, and microwave on high for about 30 seconds.

Prep: 30 minutes **Bake:** 30 minutes **Oven:** 300°F
Makes: 36 pieces

- 1   cup dry-roasted cashews
- ½   cup coarsely chopped macadamia nuts
- ½   cup flaked coconut
- ⅓   cup coarsely chopped dried pineapple
- ⅓   cup coarsely chopped dried papaya
- ⅓   cup coarsely chopped dried apricots
- ⅓   cup golden raisins
- 1   teaspoon ground cinnamon
- ⅔   cup all-purpose flour
- ½   cup honey
- ⅓   cup granulated sugar
- 1   tablespoon powdered sugar

1. Preheat oven to 300°F. Grease an 8×8×2-inch baking pan. Line pan with parchment paper, extending paper over edges of pan; grease paper. Set baking pan aside.

2. Combine cashews, macadamia nuts, coconut, pineapple, papaya, apricots, raisins, and cinnamon in a large bowl. Add flour; toss to coat.

3. Combine honey and granulated sugar in a small saucepan. Cook and stir on low heat until sugar dissolves. Bring to boiling. Reduce heat; simmer, uncovered, for 2 minutes. Quickly stir syrup into nut mixture with a wooden spoon until mixture is well coated. Quickly spread mixture in prepared pan. Lightly press mixture evenly in pan with the back of the wooden spoon or spatula.

4. Bake for 30 minutes. Cool completely in pan on a wire rack. Use parchment paper to lift mixture out of pan. Cut mixture into 9 squares, then cut each square into 4 triangles. Sprinkle with powdered sugar.

Per piece: 88 cal., 4 g total fat (1 g sat. fat), 0 mg chol., 35 mg sodium, 14 g carbo., 1 g fiber, 1 g pro.

Nut and Chocolate Bark

Chocolate candy coating provides the creamy, velvety texture of real chocolate, but it does not require tempering and it sets up more quickly.

Prep: 25 minutes **Chill:** 1 hour **Makes:** 20 servings
(1¼ pounds)

- Butter
- 8   ounces chocolate-flavor candy coating, cut up
- 4   ounces milk chocolate bar, cut up
- 1¾   cups cashews, almonds, hazelnuts (filberts), or pecans, toasted and chopped (see note, page 24)

1. Line a large baking sheet with foil; lightly butter foil. Set baking sheet aside.

2. Heat and stir candy coating and milk chocolate in a heavy medium saucepan on low heat until melted and smooth. Remove from heat. Stir in the nuts; mix well. Pour mixture onto prepared baking sheet. Spread to about ¼-inch thickness.

3. Use foil to lift firm candy from baking sheet; carefully break candy into pieces.

Per serving: 165 cal., 11 g total fat (5 g sat. fat), 2 mg chol., 8 mg sodium, 14 g carbo., 1 g fiber, 2 g pro.

Fruited Nut and Chocolate Bark: Prepare Nut and Chocolate Bark as directed, using almonds, hazelnuts (filberts), or pecans and stirring in ⅔ cup dried cranberries or cherries with the nuts.

Candied Orange and Walnut Bark: Prepare Nut and Chocolate Bark as directed, except substitute chopped toasted walnuts for the other nuts and stir in ⅓ cup diced candied orange peel.

S'more Bark: Prepare Nut and Chocolate Bark as directed, except substitute ⅔ cup salted peanuts or the other nuts and fold in ⅔ cup tiny marshmallows and ⅔ cup chopped graham cracker sticks.

Easy Cocoa Fudge

There is no need to use a candy thermometer or to engage in vigorous stirring with this foolproof, easy-does-it recipe.

Prep: 25 minutes **Chill:** 2 hours
Makes: 64 pieces or about 1¾ pounds

- 1   **16-ounce package (4 cups) powdered sugar**
- ½   **cup unsweetened European-style (Dutch- process) cocoa powder or unsweetened cocoa powder**
- ½   **cup butter**
- ¼   **cup water**
- ½   **cup buttermilk powder or nonfat dry milk powder**
- 1   **teaspoon vanilla**
- ½   **cup chopped walnuts or pecans (optional)**

Easy Cocoa Fudge

1. Line an 8×8×2-inch baking pan with foil, extending foil over edges of pan. Butter foil; set aside.

2. In a large mixing bowl sift together powdered sugar and cocoa powder. (If mixture seems lumpy, sift again.)

3. In a small saucepan combine ½ cup butter and water. Cook on medium heat until butter is just melted. Whisk in buttermilk powder. Continue cooking on medium heat just to boiling, whisking mixture until smooth. Remove pan from heat. Whisk in vanilla. Stir melted butter mixture into the powdered sugar mixture. Add chopped nuts, if desired, stirring until well combined.

4. Immediately turn fudge mixture into the prepared pan. Using your hands, press mixture evenly into pan. While fudge is warm, score it into 1-inch squares. Cover and chill for 2 to 3 hours or until firm.

5. When fudge is firm, use foil to lift it out of pan. Cut fudge into squares. Store tightly covered in the refrigerator for up to 1 month.

Per piece: 48 cal., 2 g total fat (1 g sat. fat), 5 mg chol., 20 mg sodium, 8 g carbo., 0 g fiber, 1 g pro.

Pralines

Leftover pralines may be finely ground and stirred into mousses, ice creams, and icings.

Prep: 30 minutes **Cook:** 16 minutes
Cool: 30 minutes
Makes: 1¾ pounds (about 36 pieces)

Butter
- 1½   **cups granulated sugar**
- 1½   **cups packed brown sugar**
- 1   **cup half-and-half or light cream**
- 3   **tablespoons butter**
- 2   **cups toasted pecan halves or pieces (see note, page 24)**

1. Line a baking sheet with waxed paper; set aside. Butter the sides of a heavy 2-quart saucepan. Combine granulated sugar, brown sugar, and half-

and-half in saucepan. Cook and stir on medium-high heat until mixture boils. Clip a candy thermometer to side of pan. Reduce heat to medium-low. Continue boiling mixture at a moderate, steady rate, stirring occasionally, for 16 to 18 minutes or until thermometer registers 234°F, soft-ball stage. (Adjust heat as necessary to maintain a steady boil.)

2. Remove pan from heat. Add 3 tablespoons butter; do not stir. Cool, without stirring, about 30 minutes or until thermometer registers 150°F.

3. Remove thermometer from saucepan. Stir in pecans. Beat vigorously with a clean wooden spoon about 3 minutes or just until mixture begins to thicken but is still glossy.

4. Working quickly, drop praline mixture from a teaspoon onto the prepared baking sheet. Let stand at room temperature until firm.

Per praline: 125 cal., 6 g total fat (1 g sat. fat), 5 mg chol.,17 mg sodium, 18 g carbo., 1 g fiber, 1 g pro.

Classic Butter Toffee

Classic Butter Toffee

At the beginning of the candymaking season, be sure to test your candy thermometer for accuracy by immersing its tip in boiling water for 3 minutes. If it does not read 212°F, make adjustments.

Prep: 15 minutes **Cook:** 15 minutes
Stand: 3 minutes **Chill:** 20 minutes
Makes: about 1½ pounds

Butter
1 **cup butter**
1 **cup sugar**
3 **tablespoons water**
1 **tablespoon light-color corn syrup**
1 **teaspoon vanilla**
1 **cup bittersweet or semisweet chocolate pieces**

1. Line a 13×9×2-inch baking pan with foil, extending foil over edges of pan. Set pan aside.

2. Butter the sides of a heavy 2-quart saucepan. Melt 1 cup butter in the saucepan. Add sugar,

water, and corn syrup. Cook and stir on medium-high heat until mixture boils. Clip a candy thermometer to side of pan. Reduce heat to medium; continue boiling at a moderate, steady rate, stirring frequently, until thermometer registers 290°F, soft-crack stage (about 15 minutes). Adjust heat as necessary to maintain a steady boil. Watch syrup carefully after it reaches 280°F to prevent scorching. Remove saucepan from heat; remove thermometer. Stir in vanilla. Pour candy into the prepared pan, spreading quickly to an even thickness of about ¼ inch. (Toffee will not cover entire surface of prepared pan.)

3. Let candy stand for 2 to 3 minutes or just until set. Sprinkle with chocolate pieces. Let stand for 1 to 2 minutes. When chocolate pieces have softened, spread melted chocolate over candy. Chill in refrigerator about 20 minutes or until candy is firm.

4. Use foil to lift candy out of pan. Break candy in 2-inch pieces.

Per piece: 139 cal., 11 g total fat (7 g sat. fat), 21 mg chol., 56 mg sodium, 13 g carbo., 1 g fiber, 0 g pro.

Doubly Decadent Truffles

Doubly Decadent Truffles

When chilling truffles, be sure that there are no strong-smelling foods—such as onions or cabbage—in the fridge. The chocolate may absorb their odors.

Prep: 30 minutes **Chill:** 3 hours + 10 minutes
Makes: about 48 truffles

14 **ounces premium dark baking chocolate, chopped**
¾ **cup whipping cream**
2 **tablespoons butter**
1 **tablespoon raspberry-flavor liqueur**
10 **ounces milk chocolate or semisweet chocolate, chopped**
2 **tablespoons shortening**
2 **ounces premium dark baking chocolate, melted***

1. Microwave the 14 ounces premium dark chocolate, cream, and butter in a large microwave-safe bowl on medium for 2 to 2½ minutes or until mixture is melted and smooth, stirring 3 times during cooking. Stir in liqueur. Cover and chill mixture for 1½ to 2 hours or until almost firm.

2. Line a baking sheet with waxed paper. Shape chocolate mixture into 1-inch balls using a 1-inch scoop or 2 teaspoons; place on the prepared baking sheet (mixture will be sticky; balls will be irregularly shaped). Chill about 1 hour or until firm.

3. Microwave milk chocolate and shortening in a medium microwave-safe bowl on medium for 1½ to 2 minutes or until mixture is melted and smooth, stirring twice. Dip balls, one at a time, into melted chocolate mixture. Let excess chocolate mixture drip back into bowl. Place truffles on baking sheet lined with waxed paper. Chill about 30 minutes or until set.

4. Place the 2 ounces melted premium dark baking chocolate in a resealable plastic bag; seal bag. Snip off a tiny corner of the bag. Drizzle chocolate over truffles in a crisscross design. Chill truffles about 10 minutes or until chocolate is set.

***Note:** To melt the 2 ounces premium dark chocolate, chop chocolate and microwave in a small microwave-safe bowl on medium for 1 to 2 minutes or until melted and smooth, stirring once.

Per truffle: 105 cal., 7 g total fat (4 g sat. fat), 8 mg chol., 21 mg sodium, 9 g carbo., 1 g fiber, 1 g pro.

Peanutty Brittle

The last-minute addition of baking soda is responsible for giving brittle its finely honeycombed texture.

Start to Finish: 30 minutes **Makes:** 32 servings (about 2 pounds)

Butter
2 cups sugar
1 cup light-color corn syrup
2½ cups salted peanuts
2 tablespoons butter
2 teaspoons vanilla
2 teaspoons baking soda, sifted

1. Butter a large baking sheet; set baking sheet aside. Combine sugar and corn syrup in a microwave-safe 8-cup glass measure. Microwave, uncovered, on high for 5 to 7 minutes or until sugar is dissolved and mixture is bubbly over entire surface, stirring twice.*

2. Add peanuts; stir to combine. Microwave mixture, uncovered, on high for 4 minutes. Stir in 2 tablespoons butter and the vanilla. Cook, uncovered, on high for 3 to 4 minutes more or until the candy reaches hard-crack stage (295°F to 305°F)** and syrup is a clear, golden color. After 2 minutes of cooking, stir peanut mixture after every 30 seconds.

3. Stir in baking soda. Immediately pour mixture onto the prepared baking sheet, spreading the mixture as thinly as possible.

4. Cool brittle completely. Break it into pieces.

***Note:** Sugar mixture will be extremely hot. To avoid burning yourself, use a hot pad when moving the glass measure because even the handle on the glass measure gets hot. To avoid breakage, be sure the glass measure contains no hairline cracks. Place the hot glass measure on a wooden or heat-resistant plastic cutting board rather than on granite, marble, or a surface that discolors from heat. Completely cool the glass measure before pouring water into it to soak.

****Note:** To check doneness without a thermometer, spoon a few drops of the hot candy mixture (without nuts) into a cup of cold (but not icy) water. Using your fingers, attempt to form the candy mixture into a ball and remove it from the water. The candy should not form a ball but should separate into hard, brittle threads that snap easily.

To store: Place candy in layers separated by pieces of waxed paper in an airtight container; cover. Store at room temperature for up to 2 weeks or freeze for up to 3 months. Thaw candy, if frozen, before serving.

Per piece: 137 cal., 6 g total fat (1 g sat. fat), 2 mg chol., 90 mg sodium, 19 g carbo., 1 g fiber, 3 g pro.

Peanutty Brittle

gifts. to give

When you're looking for something special to give this season, look no farther than your very own kitchen. There you can pour your heart into the pleasure of making one of these superlative sweets or savory surprises—each a personalized gift and each made with love.

Lemony Gingerbread People, page 129

1. Preheat oven to 350°F. Line a 13×9×2-inch baking pan with foil; lightly grease the foil. Spread nuts in an even layer in the prepared pan. In a small bowl combine Worcestershire-style marinade, oil, thyme, rosemary, salt, and cayenne pepper. Drizzle over nuts; toss gently to coat.

2. Bake for 12 to 15 minutes or until nuts are toasted and appear dry, stirring occasionally. Spread nuts on a large sheet of foil; cool completely.

To store: Store in an airtight container at room temperature for up to 3 weeks.

Per ¼ cup: 242 cal., 19 g total fat (1 g sat. fat), 0 mg chol., 132 mg sodium, 8 g carbo., 4 g fiber, 8 g pro.

Scottish Oat Bites with Stilton

These buttery whole grain bites are absolutley irresistible.

Prep: 40 minutes **Bake:** 8 minutes **Oven:** 375°F
Makes: about 48 crackers

- 1 cup quick-cooking rolled oats
- ¾ cup all-purpose flour
- ½ cup whole wheat flour
- 2 tablespoons toasted wheat germ or wheat bran
- 1 teaspoon salt
- 1 teaspoon baking powder
- ½ cup cold butter, cut up
- 3 ounces Stilton or other blue-veined cheese, crumbled
- ⅓ cup milk
- 1 tablespoon honey

1. Preheat oven to 375°F. Lightly grease baking sheets; set aside. Place oats in a blender or food processor; cover and blend or process until coarsely ground.

2. In a large bowl combine ground oats, all-purpose flour, whole wheat flour, wheat germ, salt, and baking powder. Using a pastry blender, cut in butter and Stilton until pieces are pea size.

Savory Nuts

Lucky recipients will especially appreciate a gift of healthful nuts during this sweet-filled time of year.

Prep: 10 minutes **Bake:** 12 minutes **Oven:** 350°F
Makes: 8 (¼-cup) servings

- 2 cups whole almonds, pecan halves, and/or cashews
- 2 tablespoons Worcestershire-style marinade for chicken
- 1 tablespoon olive oil
- 2 teaspoons snipped fresh thyme or ½ teaspoon dried thyme, crushed
- 1 teaspoon snipped fresh rosemary or ¼ teaspoon dried rosemary, crushed
- ¼ teaspoon salt
- ⅛ teaspoon cayenne pepper

3. In a small bowl combine milk and honey, stirring until honey is dissolved. Drizzle honey mixture over flour mixture; toss together with a fork. Gently work mixture with your fingers until mixture clings together.

4. Turn dough out onto a lightly floured surface. Knead for two or three turns or until dough is smooth. Divide dough in half.

5. On a lightly floured surface, roll one dough half to about 1/8-inch thickness. Using a 2- to 2 1/2-inch cookie cutter, cut out shapes and arrange on prepared baking sheets. Repeat with remaining dough, rerolling as needed.

6. Bake for 8 to 10 minutes or until edges are lightly browned. Transfer to a wire rack to cool.

To store: Prepare and bake as directed. Layer cooled crackers between sheets of waxed paper in an airtight container; cover. Freeze for up to 1 month. Thaw at room temperature.

Per cracker: 44 cal., 3 g total fat (2 g sat. fat), 6 mg chol., 95 mg sodium, 4 g carbo., 0 g fiber, 1 g pro.

Marinated Olives

Marinated Olives

If you intend to marinate olives for multiple gifts, be sure to check the prices on gallon or half-gallon jars at your local discount center—their prices are often half that of the smaller retail-size jars.

Prep: 10 minutes **Chill:** 2 days **Stand:** 1 hour
Makes: 2 cups olives (8 to 10 servings)

  2 **cups black and/or green olives, pitted, rinsed, and drained**
 1/2 **cup extra virgin olive oil**
  2 **3×1/2-inch strips of lemon peel**
 1/2 **cup lemon juice**
  4 **to 6 cloves garlic, sliced**
  2 **teaspoons snipped fresh oregano or 1 teaspoon dried oregano, crushed**
  1 **bay leaf**
 1/2 **teaspoon crushed red pepper**

1. In a 1-quart jar with a screw-top lid combine olives, olive oil, lemon peel, lemon juice, garlic, oregano, bay leaf, and red pepper. Cover and shake to coat olives with marinade. Refrigerate for 2 days, shaking jar occasionally.

2. Let jar stand at room temperature for 1 to 2 hours before serving. Remove olives from marinade to serve. Store in the refrigerator for up to 2 weeks.

Per serving: 69 cal., 7 g total fat (1 g sat. fat), 0 mg chol., 293 mg sodium, 2 g carbo., 1 g fiber, 0 g pro.

Wake-Up Cocoa Mix

Dolled up in a cute cup, this chocolatey mix makes an ideal—and affordable—gift for your children's favorite teachers.

Start to Finish: 10 minutes
Makes: 4 cups mix (13 servings)

1¾ cups nonfat dry milk powder
1 cup sifted powdered sugar
½ cup powdered fat-free nondairy creamer
⅓ cup sifted unsweetened cocoa powder
2 cups miniature marshmallows
Miniature marshmallows (optional)

1. For mix, in a medium bowl combine dry milk powder, powdered sugar, nondairy creamer, and cocoa powder. Stir in the 2 cups marshmallows. Store in an airtight container at room temperature for up to 3 months.

2. For each serving, place ⅓ cup of the cocoa mix in a cup. Add ¾ cup boiling water; stir well. If desired, top with additional miniature marshmallows.

Per serving: 165 cal., 3 g total fat (1 g sat. fat), 3 mg chol., 861 mg sodium, 30 g carbo., 0 g fiber, 4 g pro.

Peppermint Cocoa: Prepare mix as directed. For each serving, place ⅓ cup of the cocoa mix and 1½ teaspoons finely crushed peppermint candy in a cup. Add ¾ cup boiling water. Stir well. If desired, top with additional miniature marshmallows and finely crushed peppermint candy.

Wake-Up Cocoa Mix

Mocha Hot Cocoa Mix

Go over the river and through the woods with a supply of this luscious brew in tow—you'll be the most welcome houseguest ever.

Start to Finish: 15 minutes
Makes: 5 (3-serving) bags

3 cups nonfat dry milk powder
1½ cups sifted powdered sugar
1½ cups unsweetened cocoa powder
⅔ cup instant coffee crystals
1 teaspoon salt
1 cup miniature semisweet chocolate pieces

1. In a bowl stir together milk powder, powdered sugar, cocoa powder, coffee crystals, and salt. Divide mixture among 5 gift bags. Sprinkle some of the chocolate pieces into each bag. Seal and store at room temperature for up to 3 months.

Directions to give with cocoa mix: Stir chocolate pieces into cocoa mix. For each serving, place ⅓ cup of the mix in a mug. Add 1 cup boiling water, stirring until chocolate chips melt. If desired, top with marshmallows or whipped cream.

Per serving: 257 cal., 5 g total fat (2 g sat. fat), 5 mg chol., 287 mg sodium, 40 g carbo., 1 g fiber, 12 g pro.

Chewy Mint-Chocolate Stix

Mint and chocolate make one of the tastiest culinary combinations.

Prep: 35 minutes **Bake:** 15 minutes **Stand:** 1 hour
Oven: 350°F **Makes:** 30 cookies

1¾ cups white baking pieces
 2 tablespoons sweetened condensed milk
 ¼ teaspoon mint or peppermint extract
 ½ cup butter, softened
 ¼ cup shortening
 ½ cup packed brown sugar
 ½ teaspoon vanilla
 ¼ teaspoon salt
1¾ cups all-purpose flour
 ½ cup miniature semisweet chocolate pieces
 4 teaspoons shortening

Chewy Mint-Chocolate Stix

1. Preheat oven to 350°F. Lightly grease a cookie sheet; set aside.

2. For filling, microwave ¾ cup of the white baking pieces and the sweetened condensed milk in a small microwave-safe bowl on medium for 1 to 2 minutes or until baking pieces begin to melt, stirring twice (do not overcook or white baking pieces become grainy). Cool slightly. Stir in mint extract. (Filling will be thick.) Set aside.

3. In a large bowl beat butter and ¼ cup shortening with an electric mixer on medium to high for 30 seconds. Add brown sugar, vanilla, and salt. Beat until combined, scraping sides of bowl occasionally. Beat in as much of the flour as you can with the mixer. Stir in any remaining flour and the chocolate pieces (mixture will be crumbly). Knead until dough comes together. Shape dough into a ball.

4. Divide dough in half. Roll one dough portion between 2 sheets of waxed paper into a 12×6-inch rectangle. Remove the top sheet of waxed paper. Evenly pat half of the filling lengthwise over half of the dough to within ½ inch of edges. Carefully fold dough rectangle lengthwise in half to cover the filling, using the waxed paper to lift the dough; seal all edges. Repeat with remaining dough and filling. Carefully invert filled dough rectangles onto prepared cookie sheet, using the waxed paper

to flip the dough. Peel away the waxed paper and discard. Make sure all edges of dough rectangles are sealed.

5. Bake for 15 to 20 minutes or until edges are lightly brown. Cool on cookie sheet on a wire rack. Transfer baked rectangles to a cutting board; cut crosswise into ¾-inch-wide strips.

6. Microwave remaining 1 cup white baking pieces and the 4 teaspoons shortening in a small microwave-safe bowl on medium for 1½ to 2 minutes or until mixture is melted and smooth, stirring two or three times. Transfer melted mixture to a shallow container that is at least 7 inches wide. Dip one long side of each cookie into the melted mixture. Place cookies, dipped side up, on waxed paper; let stand about 1 hour or until set.

To store: Place cookies in layers separated by pieces of waxed paper in an airtight container; cover. Store at room temperature for up to 3 days or freeze for up to 3 months. Thaw cookies, if frozen, before serving.

Per cookie: 142 cal., 8 g total fat (8 g sat. fat), 12 mg chol., 61 mg sodium, 15 g carbo., 0 g fiber, 2 g pro.

Minty Cocoa Fudge Sandwich Cookies

1. In a medium bowl combine flour, cocoa powder, and baking powder; set aside.

2. In a large bowl beat butter with an electric mixer on medium to high for 30 seconds. Add the 1½ cups sugar and the oil. Beat until well mixed. Add eggs and vanilla; beat until combined. Add flour mixture; beat until combined. Cover and chill about 1 hour or until dough is easy to handle.

3. Preheat oven to 350°F. Shape dough into 1-inch balls. Place balls 2 inches apart on an ungreased cookie sheet. Dip the bottom of a glass in additional sugar and flatten each cookie. Bake for 7 to 9 minutes or just until firm. Transfer cookies to a wire rack and let cool.

4. For filling, in a small saucepan combine sweetened condensed milk, chocolate pieces, and unsweetened chocolate. Cook and stir over medium heat until melted and smooth. Remove from heat. Let stand about 1 hour or until cool.

5. On the flat side of half the cookies, spoon a rounded measuring teaspoon of the filling. Top with remaining cookies, flat sides down, pressing lightly together.

*Note: If you can't find mint-flavor semisweet chocolate pieces, use 1½ cups regular semisweet chocolate pieces and stir ¼ teaspoon mint extract into the melted chocolate mixture.

Per sandwich cookie: 247 cal., 14 g total fat (8 g sat. fat), 34 mg chol., 90 mg sodium, 32 g carbo., 1 g fiber, 3 g pro.

Minty Cocoa Fudge Sandwich Cookies

These superlative sandwiches say "I love you" in a most delicious way.

Prep: 30 minutes **Chill:** 1 hour
Bake: 7 minutes per batch **Stand:** 1 hour
Oven: 350°F **Makes:** about 36 sandwich cookies

- 3½ **cups all-purpose flour**
- ⅔ **cup unsweetened Dutch-process cocoa powder or unsweetened cocoa powder**
- 2 **teaspoons baking powder**
- 1⅓ **cups butter, softened**
- 1½ **cups sugar**
- ¼ **cup cooking oil**
- 2 **eggs**
- 1 **tablespoon vanilla**
-   **Sugar**
- 1 **14-ounce can sweetened condensed milk**
- 1 **10-ounce package mint-flavor semisweet chocolate pieces***
- 2 **ounces unsweetened chocolate, coarsely chopped**

Easy Cinnamon Spirals

This is a great recipe for getting kids involved in the kitchen. Think how proud they'll be when they deliver goodies they've prepared themselves.

Prep: 30 minutes **Bake:** 12 minutes
Oven: 375°F **Makes:** 12 rolls

-   **Nonstick cooking spray**
- 2 **11-ounce packages (12 each) refrigerated breadsticks**
- ⅓ **cup butter, softened**

¼ cup sugar
2 teaspoons ground cinnamon
½ cup caramel ice cream topping

1. Preheat oven to 375°F. Lightly coat twelve 2½-inch muffin cups with cooking spray; set aside. Unroll and separate breadsticks. Press each piece of dough to flatten slightly. Press short ends of 2 strips together to make 1 long strip. Spread strips with some of the butter.

2. In a small bowl stir together sugar and cinnamon. Sprinkle sugar mixture over each strip. Roll up each strip into a spiral. Place spirals in prepared muffin cups, spiral sides up.

3. Bake for 12 to 15 minutes or until golden. Remove from muffin cups and place on a serving plate. While warm, drizzle with caramel topping.

Per roll: 246 cal., 8 g total fat (5 g sat. fat), 14 mg chol., 443 mg sodium, 40 g carbo., 1 g fiber, 4 g pro.

Lemony Gingerbread People

Seldom-used spices lose potency during storage. For the best flavor, replace baking spices every year.

Prep: 30 minutes **Chill:** 3 hours **Bake:** 8 minutes
Oven: 350°F **Makes:** about 12 cookies

2 cups all-purpose flour
½ cup whole wheat flour
¾ teaspoon baking soda
½ teaspoon ground cinnamon
½ teaspoon ground cloves
½ cup butter, softened
½ cup sugar
⅓ cup molasses
1 egg
1 tablespoon grated fresh ginger
2 teaspoons finely shredded lemon peel
1 recipe Lemony Powdered Sugar Icing
  Tiny decorative candies or raisins
  (optional)

1. In a medium bowl combine all-purpose flour, whole wheat flour, baking soda, cinnamon, and cloves; set aside.

2. In a large bowl beat butter with an electric mixer on medium to high for 30 seconds. Add sugar; beat until combined. Add molasses and egg; beat until combined. Beat in as much of the flour mixture as you can with the mixer. Using a wooden spoon, stir in any remaining flour mixture, the ginger, and lemon peel. Divide dough in half. Cover and chill dough about 3 hours or until easy to handle.

3. Preheat oven to 350°F. Grease a cookie sheet; set aside. On a lightly floured surface, roll one portion of dough to ¼ inch thickness. Using 4½- to 6-inch gingerbread cutters, cut out dough. Place cutouts 1 inch apart on prepared cookie sheet.

4. Bake for 8 to 10 minutes or until edges are firm. Cool cookies on cookie sheet for 1 minute. Transfer cookies to a wire rack and let cool.

5. Decorate cookies with Lemony Powdered Sugar Icing and, if desired, candies or raisins.

Lemony Powdered Sugar Icing: In a small bowl combine 2 cups powdered sugar, 1 tablespoon milk, 2 teaspoons lemon juice, and ½ teaspoon vanilla. Stir in additional milk, 1 teaspoon at a time, until icing reaches piping consistency. (Or for a glaze, thin icing with additional milk, adding 1 teaspoon at a time, until icing reaches desired consistency. Spoon over cookies.)

Make-ahead directions and storing: Prepare, bake, and cool cookies as directed. Layer uniced cookies between sheets of waxed paper in an airtight container; cover. Store at room temperature for up to 3 days or freeze for up to 3 months. Thaw cookies, if frozen. Decorate with Lemony Powdered Sugar Icing and candies as desired.

Per cookie: 305 cal., 8 g total fat (5 g sat. fat), 38 mg chol., 144 mg sodium, 55 g carbo., 1 g fiber, 4 g pro.

Giant Coconut Macaroons

These massive macaroons are a coconut lover's dream come true.

Prep: 30 minutes **Bake:** 20 minutes
Stand: 30 minutes **Oven:** 325°F
Makes: about 28 cookies

4	egg whites
1	teaspoon vanilla
¼	teaspoon cream of tartar
⅛	teaspoon salt
1 ⁄3	cups sugar
1	14-ounce package flaked coconut

1. Preheat oven to 325°F. Line cookie sheets with parchment paper; set aside. In a very large mixing bowl beat egg whites, vanilla, cream of tartar, and salt with an electric mixer on high until soft peaks form (tips curl). Gradually add sugar, about 1 tablespoon at a time, beating until stiff peaks form (tips stand straight). Fold in coconut, half at a time.

2. Use a 2-inch-diameter ice cream scoop (#20 scoop or about 3 tablespoons) to drop coconut mixture into mounds on the prepared cookie sheets, leaving about 1 inch between mounds. Place cookie sheets on separate oven racks. Bake for 20 minutes. Turn off oven; let cookies dry in oven for 30 minutes. Transfer cookies to a wire rack and let cool.

Per cookie: 106 cal., 5 g total fat (4 g sat. fat), 0 mg chol., 56 mg sodium, 15 g carbo., 1 g fiber, 1 g pro.

For smaller cookies: Preheat oven to 325°F. Drop mixture from a teaspoon into small mounds on parchment paper-lined baking sheet. Bake 20 minutes or until cookies are lightly browned. Dry in oven and cool as above. Makes about 60 cookies.

Giant Coconut Macaroons

Tiramisu Biscotti

Every incredibly crisp bite of these Italian-inspired bicotti is filled with the taste of tantalizing tiramisu.

Prep: 40 minutes **Chill:** 1 hour
Bake: 25 minutes + 18 minutes **Cool:** 1 hour
Oven: 350°F/325°F **Makes:** about 30 cookies

2	tablespoons whipping cream
1	tablespoon instant espresso coffee powder or 2 tablespoons instant coffee granules
⅓	cup butter, softened
1	cup sugar
1½	teaspoons baking powder
¼	teaspoon salt
2	eggs
1	teaspoon vanilla
2¼	cups all-purpose flour
½	cup finely chopped semisweet chocolate (about 3 ounces)
1½	teaspoons finely shredded orange peel (optional)
6	ounces semisweet chocolate, coarsely chopped
1	tablespoon shortening
2	ounces white chocolate or white chocolate baking squares, coarsely chopped
2	teaspoons shortening

Tiramisu Biscotti

1. Preheat oven to 350°F. Lightly grease two cookie sheets; set aside. In a small bowl combine whipping cream and instant espresso powder until powder is dissolved; set aside.

2. In a large bowl beat butter with an electric mixer on medium to high for 30 seconds. Add sugar, baking powder, and salt. Beat until combined, scraping sides of bowl occasionally. Beat in espresso mixture, eggs, and vanilla until combined. Beat in as much of the flour as you can. Using a wooden spoon, stir in any remaining flour, the finely chopped semisweet chocolate, and, if using, the orange peel. Wrap dough in plastic wrap and chill about 1 hour or until easy to handle.

3. Shape chilled dough into two 9-inch-long rolls. Place rolls on prepared cookie sheets; flatten slightly until about 2 inches wide.

4. Bake for 25 minutes or until a toothpick inserted into a crack in dough near the center comes out clean. Cool on cookie sheets for 1 hour.

5. Reduce oven temperature to 325°F. Using a serrated knife, cut each baked loaf diagonally into ½-inch-thick slices. Bake for 10 minutes. Turn slices over. Bake for 8 to 10 minutes more or until dry and crisp. Do not overbake. Transfer to a wire rack to cool.

6. In a small saucepan cook and stir coarsely chopped semisweet chocolate and the 1 tablespoon shortening over low heat until chocolate is melted. Dip the bottom edge of each cookie into the chocolate mixture. Let dry on waxed paper.

7. In a saucepan cook and stir white chocolate and the 2 teaspoons shortening over low heat until melted. Drizzle melted white chocolate mixture over tops of cookies. Let dry on waxed paper.

Per biscotti: 144 cal., 7 g total fat (4 g sat. fat), 21 mg chol., 60 mg sodium, 21 g carbo., 1 g fiber, 2 g pro.

new year's bash

The beginning of a new year prompts many people to list the ways they intend to do better in the coming months. This time around vow to be the best cook you can be—and begin by cooking party fare like this.

Citrus-Raspberry Cooler

Citrus-Raspberry Cooler

Every holiday party should include a nonalcoholic beverage option. This one is ravishingly refreshing.

Prep: 15 minutes **Chill:** 2 hours
Makes: 12 (8-ounce) servings

- 2 **cups water**
- ⅓ **cup sugar**
- 5 **raspberry-flavored herbal tea bags**
- 1 **6-ounce can frozen orange juice concentrate, thawed**
- 2 **1-liter bottles red raspberry-flavored sparkling water, chilled**
  Ice cubes
  Fresh raspberries (optional)

1. In small saucepan combine water and sugar. Bring to boiling, stirring to dissolve sugar. Remove from heat. Add tea bags. Let steep for 5 minutes. Discard tea bags. Transfer mixture to a medium bowl. Stir in the orange juice concentrate. Chill until serving time.

2. To serve, pour the chilled tea mixture into a large punch bowl. Slowly pour in sparkling water; stir gently. Serve in ice-filled glasses. If desired, garnish with raspberry kabobs.

Per serving: 38 cal., 0 g total fat, 0 mg chol., 32 mg sodium, 10 g carbo., 0 g fiber, 0 g pro.

Hot Pomegranate Grog

Pomegranate juice—it's not only healthful it sparkles with Christmasy color.

Prep: 15 minutes **Cook:** 5 minutes **Cool:** 5 minutes
Makes: about 6 (8-ounce) servings

- 4 **cups pomegranate juice**
- 1 **cup water**
- ¾ **cup orange juice**
- ½ **cup lemon juice**
- ½ **cup sugar**
  Orange slices, halved (optional)

1. In a saucepan combine pomegranate juice, water, orange juice, lemon juice, and sugar. Bring to boiling. Remove from heat; let stand 5 minutes. If desired, garnish with orange slices.

Per serving: 197 cal., 0 g total fat, 0 mg chol., 9 mg sodium, 50 g carbo., 0 g fiber, 0 g pro.

Endive Satay Bites

Belgian endive has a cream-color, cigar-shape head with slightly bitter leaves.

Start to Finish: 30 minutes
Makes: about 30 appetizers

- 1 2- to 2½-pounds purchased roasted chicken
- ⅔ cup bottled peanut sauce
- 2 tablespoons lime juice
- 1 tablespoon packed brown sugar
- ¼ cup snipped fresh cilantro
- ¼ cup honey-roasted peanuts, chopped
- 3 to 4 heads Belgian endive, separated into leaves (about 30)

1. Remove and discard skin from chicken. Pull meat from bones, discarding bones. Chop chicken (about 3 cups). Place chopped chicken in a bowl.

2. In a bowl combine peanut sauce, lime juice, brown sugar, snipped cilantro, and peanuts. Stir in chicken. Spoon mixture onto endive leaves.

Per appetizer: 77 cal., 5 g total fat (1 g sat. fat), 27 mg chol., 310 mg sodium, 3 g carbo., 0 g fiber, 6 g pro.

Chèvre-Fig Spread

Sticky figs may be difficult to snip. To make it easier, spray your kitchen shears with nonstick baking spray.

Start to Finish: 25 minutes
Makes: 12 (2-tablespoon) servings

- ¾ cup snipped dried figs
- ¾ cup crumbled chèvre (goat cheese) (3 ounces)
- ½ cup light sour cream
- 3 tablespoons snipped fresh basil
- 2 tablespoons milk
- 1 tablespoon snipped fresh thyme
   Salt
   Black pepper
- ½ cup chopped walnuts, toasted
   Toasted baguette slices or crackers

1. In a small bowl pour boiling water over figs to cover; let stand 15 minutes. Drain well.

2. In a bowl stir together chèvre, sour cream, basil, milk, and thyme. Season to taste with salt and pepper. Stir in drained figs and half the walnuts. Cover and chill in refrigerator up to 24 hours. Transfer to serving bowl. Sprinkle with remaining walnuts. Serve with baguette slices or crackers.

Per serving dip only: 100 cal., 7 g total fat (3 g sat. fat), 10 mg chol., 45 mg sodium, 8 g carbo., 1 g fiber, 4 g pro.

Hot Pomegranate Grog

Mushroom-Cheese Appetizer Bundles

When you wish to give your soiree elegant flair, serving a phyllo appetizer will make quite an impression.

Prep: 40 minutes **Bake:** 10 minutes per batch
Oven: 375°F **Makes:** 36 bundles

1½ cups chopped fresh mushrooms
1 tablespoon butter
1 5.2-ounce container semisoft cheese with garlic and herb
½ of a 3-ounce package cream cheese, softened
1 teaspoon Worcestershire sauce
⅓ cup chopped walnuts, toasted (see note, page 24)
12 sheets frozen phyllo dough (14×9-inch rectangles), thawed
½ cup butter, melted

1. For filling, in a large skillet cook and stir mushrooms in the 1 tablespoon hot butter on medium heat for 4 to 5 minutes or until mushrooms are tender and liquid has evaporated. Set aside.

2. In a bowl beat together semisoft cheese, cream cheese, and Worcestershire sauce with an electric mixer on medium until smooth; fold in the cooked mushrooms and walnuts. Set aside.

3. Preheat oven to 375°F. Unfold phyllo dough. Place one sheet of phyllo dough on a large cutting board or work surface; brush lightly with some of the butter. (Keep remaining phyllo dough covered with plastic wrap to prevent it from drying out.) Top with another sheet of phyllo dough; brush with butter. Repeat with two more sheets of phyllo and more butter. Cut phyllo stack lengthwise into thirds. Cut crosswise into fourths.

4. Place a rounded teaspoon of the filling in the center of each square. Bring the four corners of each square together and pinch to seal. Repeat with remaining phyllo dough, butter, and filling to make a total of 36 bundles. Arrange on an ungreased baking sheet. Brush remaining butter over bundles. Bake for 10 to 12 minutes or until golden. Serve warm.

Per bundle: 62 cal., 6 g total fat (3 g sat. fat), 13 mg chol., 41 mg sodium, 2 g carbo., 0 g fiber, 1 g pro.

Mushroom-Cheese Appetizer Bundles

Coarse Mustard Brisket with Cranberry-Blackberry Sauce

Inexpensive brisket is a smart way to serve beef on a budget.

Prep: 30 minutes **Chill:** overnight **Roast:** 3 hours
Oven: 325°F **Makes:** 14 servings

2 3½- to 4-pound fresh beef briskets
2 teaspoons kosher salt
2 teaspoons smoked paprika
2 teaspoons black pepper
1 teaspoon garlic powder
1 teaspoon ground coriander
1 teaspoon dried dill
1 teaspoon crushed red pepper

2 tablespoons vegetable oil

1 8-ounce jar Dijon-style stone-ground
mustard

½ cup packed brown sugar

½ cup horseradish mustard

1 cup water or beef broth

1 recipe Cranberry-Blackberry Sauce

1. Trim fat from meat, keeping the fat in one piece as much as possible; reserve fat. In a small bowl combine salt, paprika, black pepper, garlic powder, coriander, dill, and crushed red pepper. Sprinkle both sides of meat with spice mixture. Place meat in a 15×10×1-inch baking pan. Cover and chill overnight.

2. Preheat oven to 325°F. In an extra-large skillet heat oil over medium-high heat. Add one of the briskets; cook in hot oil until brown on both sides. Remove from skillet. Repeat with the remaining brisket. Place meat on a rack in a roasting pan.

3. In a small bowl combine stone-ground mustard, brown sugar, and horseradish mustard. Spread mixture over top of meat. Top with the reserved

fat. Add the water to the roasting pan. Cover pan tightly with foil.

4. Roast about 3 hours or until meat is tender. Remove and discard fat. Thinly slice meat across the grain. Serve with Cranberry-Blackberry Sauce.

Cranberry-Blackberry Sauce: In a medium saucepan bring ½ cup water to boiling. Stir in 1½ cups fresh or frozen cranberries; cook, uncovered, about 3 minutes or until berries start to pop. Stir in 1 cup blackberries. Cook, uncovered, for 2 minutes more. In a small bowl combine ½ cup sugar, 1 tablespoon cornstarch, ¼ teaspoon salt, and ⅛ teaspoon ground allspice; add to berry mixture. Cook and stir until thickened and bubbly. Cook and stir for 2 minutes more. Cool to room temperature or chill.

Per 6-ounce serving: 465 cal., 19 g total fat (6 g sat. fat), 141 mg chol., 966 mg sodium, 19 g carbo., 1 g fiber, 48 g pro.

137

Sour Cream-Fennel Pork Tenderloins

To crush fennel, use a mortar and pestle. If you don't have one, place fennel seeds in a paper envelope and crush them with a rolling pin.

Prep: 20 minutes **Cook:** 10 minutes
Roast: 25 minutes **Oven:** 425°F **Makes:** 8 servings

- 2 medium fennel bulbs
- 2 1- to 1½-pound pork tenderloins
- 1 tablespoon snipped fresh rosemary
- 1 tablespoon fennel seeds, coarsely crushed (optional)
- 2 tablespoons olive oil
- 1 medium onion, sliced
- 6 cloves garlic, minced
- ½ cup chicken broth
- ½ cup dry vermouth or chicken broth
- ¼ cup sour cream
     Rosemary sprigs (optional)
     Sour cream (optional)

1. Preheat oven to 425°F. Trim and core fennel bulbs, reserving some of the leafy tops. Cut each fennel bulb into thin wedges; set aside. Sprinkle pork with rosemary, fennel seeds (if using), 1 teaspoon salt, and ¼ teaspoon black pepper. In a 12-inch straight-sided oven-going skillet brown pork on all sides in hot oil. Remove pork from pan; set aside.

2. Add fennel, onion, and garlic to skillet; cook 4 minutes or until lightly browned, stirring occasionally. Remove skillet from heat; add broth, vermouth, and sour cream. Return to heat. Bring to boiling. Return pork to pan; transfer to oven.

3. Roast, uncovered, 25 to 30 minutes or until slightly pink in center (155°F). Serve pork with vegetables and juices. Top with reserved fennel tips and rosemary. If desired, pass additional sour cream sprinkled with rosemary.

Per serving: 212 cal., 7 g total fat (2 g sat. fat, 0 g trans fat), 77 mg chol., 448 mg sodium, 8 g carbo., 3 g fiber, 25 g pro.

Chutney-Glazed Ham with Roasted Asparagus

Avoid hams labeled "ham and water product." These products contain additional water, which makes the ham mushy and dilutes its flavor.

Prep: 10 minutes **Roast:** 1 hour + 55 minutes
Oven: 325°F/400°F **Makes:** 8 servings

- 1 3- to 4-pound boneless cooked ham
- 1 9-ounce jar mango chutney (¾ cup)
- 2 tablespoons honey
- 1 tablespoon stone-ground mustard
- 2 pounds fresh asparagus spears, trimmed
- 2 tablespoons olive oil
    Salt and black pepper
    Fresh mint leaves

1. Preheat oven to 325°F. Place ham on a rack in a shallow roasting pan. Insert an oven-going meat thermometer into center of ham. Roast, uncovered, for 1½ hours.

2. Meanwhile, for glaze, in a bowl stir together the chutney, honey, and mustard. Using kitchen scissors, snip any large pieces of fruit.

3. Spoon about ½ cup of the glaze over the ham. Roast, uncovered, for 15 minutes more or until thermometer registers 140°F. Remove from oven and cover with foil. Increase oven temperature to 400°F. Arrange asparagus in a 15×10×1-inch baking pan. Drizzle asparagus with olive oil and sprinkle with salt and pepper; toss to coat. Roast, uncovered, for 10 minutes or until crisp-tender, stirring once.

4. Serve ham with remaining chutney mixture and asparagus. Garnish with fresh mint.

Per serving: 295 cal., 12 g total fat (2 g sat. fat), 83 mg chol., 1,637 mg sodium, 21 g carbo., 2 g fiber, 23 g pro.

Beer-Brined Turkey

Homemade brine solutions are one of the best ways to enhance the flavor and texture of meats like turkey that tend to dry as they roast.

Prep: 25 minutes **Chill:** overnight
Roast: 1¼ hours **Stand:** 15 minutes
Oven: 325°F **Makes:** 6 servings

- 1 1¾- to 2-pounds bone-in turkey breast portion
- 3 12-ounce cans beer
- 4 cloves garlic, peeled and sliced
- ¼ cup coarse salt
- 4 fresh rosemary sprigs
- 6 bay leaves
   Water
- 1 tablespoons butter, melted
- 2 cloves garlic, minced
- 1 teaspoon paprika
- 1 teaspoon dried thyme, crushed
- ½ teaspoon ground sage
- ½ teaspoon onion powder
- ¼ teaspoon black pepper

1. Place turkey in a very large bowl. Pour beer over turkey. Add sliced garlic cloves, salt, rosemary sprigs, and bay leaves. If necessary, add enough water just to cover. Cover.

2. Preheat oven to 325°F. Remove turkey from brine, discarding the brine. Place turkey on a rack in a shallow roasting pan. In a bowl stir together the butter and minced garlic; brush over roast. In another bowl stir together the paprika, thyme, sage, onion powder, and pepper; sprinkle over turkey.

3. Insert a meat thermometer into thickest part of the breast. The thermometer should not touch bone. Roast turkey, uncovered, for 1¼ to 1¾ hours or until meat thermometer registers 170°F. Cover and let stand 15 minutes before slicing.

Per serving: 198 cal., 10 g total fat (3 g sat. fat), 78 mg chol., 846 mg sodium, 1 g carbo., 1 g fiber, 25 g pro.

139

Broccoli Rabe with Garlic

Broccoli rabe—also called"Italian broccoli," and "rapini"—has a pungent, slightly bitter flavor.

Start to Finish: 20 minutes **Makes:** 12 servings

- 3 **pounds broccoli rabe**
- 2 **tablespoons olive oil**
- 6 **cloves garlic, minced**
- ¼ **cup reduced-sodium chicken broth**
- ½ **teaspoon black pepper**
- ¼ **teaspoon salt**

1. Remove large leaves and, if necessary, cut stems into 6- to 8-inch-long pieces. In a 6- to 8-quart Dutch oven cook broccoli rabe, half at a time if necessary, in a large amount of boiling water for 3 minutes. Drain well; squeeze broccoli rabe to get it dry.

2. In the same Dutch oven heat oil on medium heat. Add garlic; cook and stir for 30 seconds. Carefully add drained broccoli rabe; cook and stir for 1 minute. Add broth and cook, uncovered, until all the broth has evaporated, stirring frequently. Stir in pepper and salt. Serve immediately.

Per serving: 106 cal., 1 g total fat (1 g sat. fat), 3 mg chol., 9 mg sodium, 24 g carbo., 2 g fiber, 0 g pro.

New England Clam Chowder

Clam chowder comes in two varieties—Manhattan-style, which is clear and tomato based, and New-England-style, the creamy concoction featured here.

Start to Finish: 45 minutes
Makes: 4 (1½-cup) servings

- 1 **pint shucked clams or two 6.5-ounce cans minced clams**
- 2 **slices bacon, halved**
- 2½ **cups chopped, peeled potatoes (3 medium)**
- 1 **cup chopped onion (1 large)**
- 1 **teaspoon instant chicken bouillon granules**
- 1 **teaspoon Worcestershire sauce**
- ¼ **teaspoon dried thyme, crushed**
- ⅛ **teaspoon black pepper**
- 2 **cups milk**
- 1 **cup half-and-half or light cream**
- 2 **tablespoons all-purpose flour**

1. Chop fresh clams, if using, reserving juice; set clams aside. Strain clam juice to remove bits of shell. (Or drain canned clams, reserving juice.) Add enough water to reserved clam juice to equal 1 cup. In a saucepan cook bacon until crisp. Remove bacon, reserving 1 tablespoon drippings in pan. Drain bacon on paper towels; crumble bacon and set aside. Stir reserved 1 cup clam juice, potatoes, onion, bouillon granules, Worcestershire sauce, thyme, and pepper into saucepan. Bring to boiling; reduce heat. Simmer, covered, 15 minutes or until potatoes are tender. With back of a fork, slightly mash potatoes against the side of the pan.

3. Stir together milk, half-and-half, and flour; add to potato mixture. Cook and stir until thickened. Stir in clams. Return to boiling; reduce heat. Cook for 1 to 2 minutes more or until heated through. Sprinkle each serving with crumbled bacon.

Per serving: 376 cal., 15 g total fat (8 g sat. fat), 76 mg chol., 495 mg sodium, 35 g carbo., 2 g fiber, 24 g pro.

Broccoli Rabe with Garlic

Rosy Beet Risotto

Rosy Beet Risotto

The reduced-sodium chicken broth called for in this risotto compensates for the saltiness of the blue cheese.

Prep: 15 minutes **Roast:** 1 hour 15 minutes
Cook: 25 minutes **Cool:** 30 minutes
Oven: 350°F **Makes:** 8 servings

- 12 ounces beets (2 medium)
- 3 tablespoons olive oil
- ½ cup chopped red onion (1 medium)
- 1½ cups Arborio or short grain rice
- 2 tablespoons snipped fresh basil or
  1 teaspoon dried basil, crushed
- 2 14-ounce cans reduced-sodium chicken broth
- ½ cup crumbled blue cheese (2 ounces)
  Salt and freshly ground pepper
  Fresh basil leaves

1. Preheat oven to 350°F. Place beets in center of 18-inch square of heavy foil. Drizzle with 1 tablespoon of the olive oil. Fold together opposite edges of foil in double folds, allowing room for steam to build. Roast 75 minutes or until tender. Cool 30 minutes. Carefully open packet.

Remove beets; gently transfer liquid to measuring cup; add water to equal ½ cup. Pour liquid into medium saucepan. Cut beets in wedges.

2. In a 3-quart saucepan cook onion in remaining oil over medium heat until tender; add rice. Cook and stir 5 minutes. Stir in dried basil, if using.

3. Meanwhile, add broth to beet liquid in saucepan. Bring to boiling. Reduce heat and simmer. Carefully stir 1 cup of the hot broth into rice mixture. Cook, stirring frequently, over medium heat until liquid is absorbed. Then add ½ cup broth at a time, stirring frequently until broth is absorbed before adding more broth (about 22 minutes).

4. Stir in any remaining broth. Cook and stir just until rice is tender and creamy.

5. Add beets; heat through. Remove rice from heat; stir in half of the cheese, snipped basil (if using), and salt and pepper to taste. Sprinkle remaining cheese and basil leaves.

Per serving: 185 cal., 7 g total fat (2 g sat. fat), 5 mg chol., 441 mg sodium, 26 g carbo., 1 g fiber, 5 g pro.

Apple, Pear, and Fennel
Platter with Gorgonzola

1 **cup Gorgonzola or other blue cheese, coarsely crumbled (4 ounces)**

1. For dressing, in a screw-top jar combine balsamic vinegar, oil, and shallot. Cover and shake well.

2. Trim fennel; cut fennel bulbs in half lengthwise and remove cores. Cut crosswise into thin slices.

3. On a large serving platter arrange arugula and/or radicchio, apples, pears, and fennel. Drizzle with dressing. Sprinkle with walnuts and cheese.

Per serving: 333 cal., 23 g total fat (6 g sat. fat), 17 mg chol., 304 mg sodium, 27 g carbo., 7 g fiber, 9 g pro.

Sticky Pecan Upside-Down Baby Cakes

Bake these gooey cakes on Christmas morning—their arousing aroma will fill your home with warmth and holiday cheer.

Prep: 20 minutes **Bake:** 25 minutes
Cool: 5 minutes **Oven:** 350°F **Makes:** 12 cakes

   Nonstick spray for baking
⅔ **cup packed brown sugar**
½ **cup butter**
⅓ **cup honey**
1½ **cups coarsely chopped pecans**
1 **teaspoon finely shredded orange peel**
2½ **cups all-purpose flour**
1 **teaspoon baking powder**
½ **teaspoon baking soda**
½ **teaspoon salt**
3 **eggs**
2 **cups granulated sugar**
1 **cup cooking oil**
1 **8-ounce carton sour cream**
2 **teaspoons vanilla**

1. Preheat oven to 350°F. Lightly coat twelve 3½-inch muffin cups with nonstick spray for baking.

2. In a saucepan combine brown sugar, butter, and honey. Cook and stir on medium heat for 2 minutes or until smooth. Remove from heat. Stir in pecans and finely shredded orange peel; set aside.

Apple, Pear, and Fennel Platter with Gorgonzola

This gorgeous platter is a must for holiday buffets—especially those that also offer baked pasta dishes.

Start to Finish: 25 minutes **Makes:** 6 servings

¼ **cup balsamic vinegar**
2 **tablespoons olive oil**
2 **tablespoons minced shallot**
2 **medium fennel bulbs**
3 **cups arugula leaves and/or shredded radicchio**
2 **medium red apples, cored and thinly sliced**
2 **medium pears, cored and thinly sliced**
1 **cup broken walnuts, toasted, (see note page 24)**

3. In a bowl stir together flour, baking powder, baking soda, and salt; set aside. In a bowl combine eggs and granulated sugar. Beat on medium to high about 3 minutes or until mixture is thick and lemon color. Add oil, sour cream, and vanilla; beat until combined. Gradually add flour mixture, beating on low until smooth.

4. Place 2 tablespoons of the pecan mixture in the bottom of each muffin cup. Spoon a heaping ⅓ cup of the batter into each cup. Place muffin pans on a large foil-lined baking sheet.

5. Bake for 25 to 30 minutes or until a toothpick inserted into the centers comes out clean. Cool in muffin pans on wire racks for 5 minutes. Using a sharp knife, loosen edges of cakes from sides of muffin cups; invert onto wire racks. Spoon pecan mixture remaining in the muffin cups onto cakes. Serve warm or cool.

Per cake: 679 cal., 41 g total fat (10 g sat. fat), 83 mg chol., 271 mg sodium, 76 g carbo., 2 g fiber, 6 g pro.

Caramel-Pecan French Silk Pie

Deliver true decadence with this creamy-rich pie. To make the pretty chocolate curls, warm a chocolate bar briefly in your hand, then shave off curls with a sharp vegetable peeler.

Prep: 25 minutes **Cook:** 13 minutes
Cool: 20 minutes **Chill:** 5 hours **Oven:** 450°F
Makes: 8 to 10 servings

 1 **cup whipping cream**
 1 **cup semisweet chocolate pieces**
 ⅓ **cup butter**
 ⅓ **cup sugar**
 2 **egg yolks, lightly beaten**
 3 **tablespoons crème de cacao or**
    whipping cream
 1 **cup caramel-flavor ice cream topping**
 1 **purchased baked pastry shell**
 ¾ **cup coarsely chopped pecans or almonds,**
    toasted (see note, page 24)
 ⅔ **cup whipping cream**
    Chocolate curls (optional)

1. In a heavy medium saucepan combine the 1 cup whipping cream, chocolate pieces, butter, and sugar. Cook on low heat about 10 minutes or until chocolate melts, stirring constantly. Remove saucepan from heat. Gradually stir half of the hot mixture into the beaten egg yolks. Return egg mixture to saucepan. Cook on medium-low heat about 5 minutes, stirring constantly, until mixture is slightly thickened and begins to bubble. Remove from heat. (Mixture may appear to separate.) Stir in crème de cacao. Place the saucepan in a bowl of ice water about 20 minutes, stirring occasionally, until mixture stiffens and becomes hard to stir.

2. Meanwhile, spread ice cream topping in bottom of baked pastry shell; sprinkle pecans evenly over ice cream topping. Transfer the cooled chocolate mixture to a bowl. Beat with on medium to high for 2 to 3 minutes or until light and fluffy. Spread chocolate mixture over pecans. Cover and chill for 5 to 24 hours.

3. In a chilled mixing bowl beat the ⅔ cup whipping cream on medium until soft peaks form. Spread over top of pie. If desired, garnish with chocolate curls.

Per serving: 727 cal., 50 g total fat (23 g sat. fat), 142 mg chol., 294 mg sodium, 70 g carbo., 3 g fiber, 7 g pro.

Caramel-Pecan
French Silk Pie

company's coming

With the help of this chapter, you'll be able to
open your door to holiday visitors with
complete confidence. These quick-fix
dishes—which will please even the pickiest
eaters—allow you to feed your guests with
grace and style, and give you time to relax
and enjoy the pleasure of their company.

Red, White, and Green Panini, page 148

Beef Stroganoff Casserole

Beef Stroganoff Casserole

Smoked paprika is ground from red chiles that have been slowly smoked and dried over oak fires. It is often labeled "Pimenton."

Prep: 35 minutes **Bake:** 30 minutes **Oven:** 350°F
Makes: 6 servings

- 12 **ounces dried campanelle or penne pasta**
- 1 **17-ounce package refrigerated cooked beef roast au jus**
- 2 **large fresh portobello mushrooms, stems removed and coarsely chopped (about 4 cups)**
- 1 **medium sweet onion, cut into thin wedges**
- 2 **cloves garlic, minced**
- 2 **tablespoons butter**
- 3 **tablespoons all-purpose flour**
- 2 **tablespoons tomato paste**
- 1 **14-ounce can beef broth**
- 1 **tablespoon Worcestershire sauce**
- 1 **teaspoon smoked paprika or Spanish paprika**
- ¼ **teaspoon salt**
- ¼ **teaspoon black pepper**
- 1 **8-ounce carton sour cream**
- 1 **tablespoon prepared horseradish**
- 1 **teaspoon snipped fresh dill or ¼ teaspoon dried dill**
    Fresh dill sprigs (optional)

1. Preheat oven to 350°F. Cook pasta according to package directions; drain. Return to hot saucepan.

2. Place roast on a cutting board; reserve juices. Using 2 forks, pull meat apart into bite-size pieces; set aside.

3. In a large skillet cook mushrooms, onion, and garlic in hot butter on medium heat for 4 to 5 minutes or until tender. Stir in flour and tomato paste. Gradually stir in meat juices, broth, Worcestershire sauce, paprika, salt, and pepper. Cook and stir until thickened and bubbly. Remove from heat. Stir in ½ cup of the sour cream.

4. Stir shredded meat and mushroom mixture into cooked pasta. Transfer mixture to an ungreased 3-quart casserole. Bake, covered, about 30 minutes or until heated through.

5. Meanwhile, in a small bowl combine the remaining sour cream, horseradish, and snipped or dried dill. Serve with stroganoff. If desired, garnish with dill sprigs.

Per serving: 485 cal., 18 g total fat (10 g sat. fat), 72 mg chol., 770 mg sodium, 56 g carbo., 4 g fiber, 26 g pro.

Three-Cheese Macaroni

Face it—kids will be kids. And they will be really good kids when this mac is on the menu.

Prep: 30 minutes **Bake:** 20 minutes
Stand: 10 minutes **Oven:** 350°F
Makes: 4 main-dish servings

- 1⅓ cups dried elbow macaroni (6 ounces)
- ¾ cup milk
- 2 tablespoons butter
- ¼ teaspoon ground white pepper
- ⅛ teaspoon salt
- 4 ounces American cheese, cut into ½-inch cubes
- 1 cup shredded sharp cheddar cheese (4 ounces)
- ¼ cup shredded mozzarella cheese (1 ounce)
   Shredded cheddar cheese (optional)

1. Preheat oven to 350°F. In a large saucepan cook macaroni according to package directions; drain. Return to saucepan.

2. Add milk, butter, pepper, and salt. Stir in cheeses. Transfer to a greased 1½-quart casserole.

3. Bake, uncovered, for 15 minutes. Carefully stir. Bake 5 minutes more or until just heated through. If desired, sprinkle with additional cheddar cheese. Let stand 10 minutes before serving.

Per serving: 474 cal., 27 g total fat (17 g sat. fat), 81 mg chol., 776 mg sodium, 35 g carbo., 1 g fiber, 22 g pro.

Blue Cheese Macaroni: Prepare as above, except omit American cheese and sharp cheddar cheese. In Step 2, stir in 1 cup (4 ounces) process Swiss cheese (shredded) and 1 cup (4 ounces) crumbled blue cheese along with the mozzarella cheese.

Three-Cheese Macaroni with Smoked Chicken: Prepare as above, except omit American cheese, sharp cheddar cheese, and mozzarella cheese. In Step 2, stir in 1 clove garlic, minced; 1 cup Asiago cheese, shredded (4 ounces); ½ cup fontina cheese, shredded (2 ounces); ¼ cup blue cheese, crumbled (1 ounce); and 1 cup chopped smoked chicken or shredded purchased roasted chicken along with the milk, butter, pepper, and salt.

Three-Cheese Macaroni

Red, White, and Green Panini

In a small bowl stir together mayonnaise and pesto; set aside.

2. Preheat an electric sandwich press, a covered indoor grill, a grill pan, or a skillet. To assemble sandwiches, place half of the provolone cheese on the bottom half of the bread loaf. Spread mayonnaise mixture over cheese. Layer with coppacola, salami, Red Onion Relish, arugula, and the remaining cheese. Replace top of loaf. Cut loaf crosswise into 4 sandwiches.

3. Place sandwiches (half at a time, if necessary) in the sandwich press or indoor grill; cover and cook about 6 minutes or until cheese melts and bread is toasted. (If using a grill pan or skillet, place sandwiches on grill pan. Weight sandwiches down and grill about 2 minutes or until bread is toasted. Turn sandwiches over, weight down, and grill until remaining side is toasted.)

Red Onion Relish: In a medium bowl combine 1 medium red onion, halved and thinly sliced (1 cup); 2 tablespoons olive oil; 1 tablespoon red wine vinegar; and 1 teaspoon snipped fresh oregano. Season to taste with salt and black pepper. Cover and let stand at room temperature for up to 2 hours. Drain before using. Makes about 1 cup.

Per sandwich: 869 cal., 54 g total fat (16 g sat. fat), 77 mg chol., 2,114 mg sodium, 63 g carbo., 4 g fiber, 32 g pro.

Red, White, and Green Panini

One panino, two panini, three panini, four—a singleItalian presssed sandwich is a panino, and group of them is panini.

Prep: 25 minutes **Grill:** 6 minutes per batch
Makes: 4 sandwiches

- 1 **recipe Red Onion Relish**
- 1 **16-ounce loaf unsliced ciabatta or Italian bread**
- 2 **tablespoons olive oil**
- ¼ **cup mayonnaise**
- 1 **tablespoon purchased basil pesto**
- 6 **ounces thinly sliced provolone cheese**
- 4 **ounces thinly sliced coppacola or cooked ham**
- 4 **ounces thinly sliced salami**
- 2 **cups fresh arugula**

1. Prepare Red Onion Relish; set aside. Cut bread in half horizontally. Brush the outside of the loaf with olive oil. Place the bottom half of the loaf on a piece of waxed paper, cut side up. Set top aside.

Smashed Potato Chowder

The addition of chopped sweet peppers takes this tater soup from blah to beautiful.

Prep: 30 minutes **Cook:** 20 minutes
Makes: 8 servings

- 3½ **pounds potatoes, peeled and cut into ¾-inch cubes**
- ¾ **cup chopped yellow or red sweet pepper (1 medium)**
- 1½ **teaspoons bottled roasted minced garlic**
- ½ **teaspoon black pepper**
- 5 **cups chicken broth**
- ½ **cup whipping cream, half-and-half, or light cream**
- 1½ **cups shredded cheddar cheese (6 ounces)**

½ **cup thinly sliced green onions (4)**
½ **cup sour cream**
½ **cup shredded cheddar cheese (2 ounces)**

1. In a 4-quart Dutch oven combine potatoes, sweet pepper, garlic, and black pepper. Add broth. Bring to boiling; reduce heat. Simmer, covered, for 20 to 25 minutes or until potatoes are tender.

2. Mash potatoes slightly with a potato masher. Stir in whipping cream, the 1½ cups shredded cheddar cheese, and green onion. Heat through. Top with sour cream and additional cheddar cheese.

Per serving: 329 cal., 18 g total fat (11 g sat. fat), 57 mg chol., 798 mg sodium, 31 g carbo., 3 g fiber, 12 g pro.

Twice-Peppered Bacon and Buttermilk Scones

Skip the crackers—savory scones turn a bowl of soup meal into a sensational treat.

Prep: 30 minutes **Bake:** 15 minutes **Oven:** 425°F
Makes: 10 scones

6 **slices bacon**
3 **medium shallots, thinly sliced**
3 **cups all-purpose flour**
1 **tablespoon baking powder**
1 **teaspoon coarsely ground black pepper**
¼ **teaspoon cayenne pepper**
½ **cup butter, cut up**
1½ **cups finely shredded Gruyère cheese (6 ounces)**
1 **cup buttermilk**
1 **egg**

1. In a large skillet cook bacon on medium heat for 8 to 10 minutes or until crisp, turning once halfway through cooking. Remove bacon from skillet; drain on paper towels. Crumble bacon; set aside. Drain fat from skillet, reserving 2 tablespoons. Cook shallots in the 2 tablespoons bacon drippings until tender; set aside.

2. Preheat oven to 425°F. Line a baking sheet with parchment paper; set aside. In a food processor combine flour, baking powder, black pepper, and cayenne pepper. Pulse food processor several times to mix. Sprinkle butter pieces over flour mixture. Pulse until mixture resembles coarse crumbs.

3. In a bowl combine the flour mixture, crumbled bacon, shallots, and Gruyère cheese. Make a well in the center of the flour mixture; set aside.

4. In a bowl whisk together buttermilk and egg. Remove 2 tablespoons of the buttermilk mixture for brushing; set aside. Add remaining buttermilk mixture all at once to the flour mixture. Using a fork, stir just until moistened.

5. Turn dough out onto a floured surface. Knead dough by folding and pressing for 10 strokes. Pat into an 8-inch circle. Cut into 10 wedges.

6. Place wedges 1 inch apart on a baking sheet lined with parchment paper. Brush with reserved 2 tablespoons buttermilk mixture. Bake for 15 minutes or until golden. Serve warm.

Per scone: 360 cal., 20 g total fat (11 g sat. fat), 73 mg chol., 381 mg sodium, 31 g carbo., 1 g fiber, 12 g pro.

Twice-Peppered Bacon and Buttermilk Scones

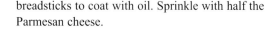

Easy Parmesan Breadsticks

Make plenty—everyone will love dipping these cheesy breadsticks into the Red Pepper Sauce.

Prep: 15 minutes **Bake:** 10 minutes **Oven:** 375°F
Makes: 12 to 15 breadsticks

1	12-ounce loaf baguette-style French bread
	Nonstick cooking spray
½	cup olive oil
¾	cup grated or finely shredded Parmesan cheese

1. Preheat oven to 375 F. Cut bread crosswise in half or into quarters. Cut each piece lengthwise in half, then into ¼- to ½-inch strips. (It is helpful to cut bread so there is crust on each strip.)

2. Line a 15×10×1-inch baking pan with foil; lightly coat with cooking spray. Arrange half the breadsticks in a single layer; drizzle with half the oil. Using a spatula or tongs, carefully turn breadsticks to coat with oil. Sprinkle with half the Parmesan cheese.

3. Bake for 10 to 12 minutes or until brown and crisp. Repeat with remaining breadsticks, oil, and cheese.

Per breadstick: 179 cal., 11 g total fat (2 g sat. fat, 4 mg chol., 249 mg sodium, 15 g carbo., 1 g fiber, 4 g pro.

Red Pepper Sauce: In a large skillet cook 4 red sweet peppers, coarsely chopped, and 2 shallots, chopped, in ¼ cup olive oil in a large skillet on medium heat about 10 minutes or until tender, stirring occasionally. Remove skillet from heat. Add ½ cup dry white wine; 4 cloves garlic, minced; 2 tablespoons snipped parsley; ½ teaspoon salt; and ¼ teaspoon black pepper. Stir to combine. Return to heat. Bring mixture to boiling; reduce heat. Cover and simmer 10 to 15 minutes until peppers are very tender. Cool slightly. Transfer to a food processor. Add 2 tablespoons snipped parsley and 2 tablespoons olive oil; cover and process until almost smooth. Makes about 1½ cups.

Caesar Salad

After using, transfer any unused anchoy fillets to a glass container, cover with 1-inch of olive oil, and refrigerate. Preserved this way, the tiny fish will keep for a year.

Prep: 30 minutes **Bake:** 20 minutes **Oven:** 300°F
Makes: 6 side-dish servings

1	recipe Parmesan Croutons
1	recipe Caesar Dressing
3	hearts of romaine, quartered lengthwise
6	canned anchovy fillets, halved lengthwise
1	ounce Parmesan cheese, shaved (optional)

1. Chill 6 salad plates. Prepare Parmesan Croutons and Caesar Dressing. To serve, place 2 romaine wedges on each plate. Drizzle with Caesar Dressing. Top each salad with 2 anchovy strips, Parmesan Croutons, and, if desired, shaved Parmesan cheese.

Caesar Salad

Crunchy Caramel Apple Cake

Parmesan Croutons: Preheat oven to 300°F. Cut four ¾-inch-thick slices Italian or French bread into 1-inch cubes (about 3½ cups); set aside. In a small saucepan melt ¼ cup butter. Remove from heat. Transfer to a large bowl. Stir in 3 tablespoons grated Parmesan cheese and 2 finely minced garlic cloves. Add bread cubes, stirring until cubes are coated with butter mixture. Spread bread cubes in a single layer in a shallow baking pan or on a baking sheet. Bake for 10 minutes; stir. Bake 10 minutes more or until bread cubes are crisp and golden. Cool completely; store in an airtight container for up to 24 hours.

Caesar Dressing: In a food processor or blender combine 3 cloves garlic, 3 canned anchovy fillets, and 2 tablespoons fresh lemon juice. Cover and blend or process until mixture is smooth, scraping sides of container as necessary. Add ¼ cup olive oil, 1 hard-cooked egg yolk, 1 teaspoon Dijon mustard, and ½ teaspoon sugar. Blend or process until smooth. Use immediately or cover and chill for up to 24 hours. Stir before using.

Per serving: 262 cal., 21 g total fat (8 g sat. fat), 65 mg chol., 521 mg sodium, 13 g carbo., 2 g fiber, 8 g pro.

Crunchy Caramel Apple Cake

Choose your favorite sweet-tart apple for this incredibly captivating cake.

Prep: 30 minutes **Bake:** 45 minutes
Oven: 325°F **Makes:** 16 servings

- 1   **cup plain granola, crushed**
- 1   **cup chopped walnuts or pecans**
- ¼   **cup butter, softened**
- 3   **cups all-purpose flour**
- 1   **teaspoon baking soda**
- 1   **teaspoon ground cinnamon**
- ½   **teaspoon salt**
- 2   **eggs**
- 1½ **cups cooking oil**
- 1   **cup granulated sugar**
- 1   **cup packed brown sugar**
- 3   **cups finely chopped, peeled apples**
- 1   **recipe Caramel Sauce**

1. Grease a 13×9×2-inch baking pan; set aside. In a medium bowl combine granola and ½ cup of the nuts. Use your fingers or a fork to combine softened butter with granola mixture until crumbly; set aside.

2. Preheat oven to 325°F. In a bowl stir together flour, baking soda, cinnamon, and salt; set aside. In a bowl beat eggs slightly with a fork; stir in oil, granulated sugar, and brown sugar. Add flour mixture; stir just until combined. Fold in apples and remaining nuts. Spoon batter into prepared pan, spreading evenly. Sprinkle with granola mixture.

3. Bake for 45 to 55 minutes or until a wooden toothpick inserted near the center comes out clean. Cool cake completely on a wire rack. Serve with warm Caramel Sauce.

Caramel Sauce: In a saucepan melt ½ cup butter on medium heat. Stir in 1 cup packed brown sugar and ½ cup whipping cream. Bring to boiling, stirring constantly; reduce heat. Simmer, uncovered, for 5 minutes or until mixture is slightly thickened. Stir in 1 teaspoon vanilla. Cool 10 minutes.

Per serving: 630 cal., 39 g total fat (10 g sat. fat), 61 mg chol., 240 mg sodium, 68 g carbo., 3 g fiber, 6 g pro.

holiday menus

Think of these menus as kits—little packets that provide everything you need to shine at holiday food festivities. With these carefully chosen menu groupings, there is no need worry about what goes with what; no reason to calculate complicated prep schedules. Just choose your favorite, and you're good to go.

menu 1

No-Panic Party

*This make-ahead menu is a snap. Prepare one dish each
night of the week. On party day, you'll be on cruise control.*

menu 2

Thanksgiving Potluck

*When you're asked to bring a dish, make it one they'll remember
you by—like one of these sensational selections.*

menu 3

Overnight Brunch

This is a clever way to go when celebrating around the tree sounds better than being stuck in the kitchen on that special morning.

menu 4

Holiday Tea

Bring the refined—and yet relaxed—British tea tradition across the pond this holiday season. It's perfect for an afternoon with the girls.

menu 5

Resolution Dinner

Or perhaps "preresolution" dinner describes it better. This fabulous feast ends the year on a rightfully rich note that serves as a last hurrah.

Triple-Onion Appetizer Tart, page 44

Sour Cream-Fennel Pork Tenderloins, page 138

Spinach Salad with Brie Toast, page 26

Creamy Brussels Sprouts with Peppered Bacon, page 18

Port Baked Pears or Apples, page 30

Turtle Cake, page 82

menu 6

Cozy Christmas Eve

Gather those you love most around a festive holiday table to savor this simple but special family feast.

New England Clam Chowder, page 140

Cheese Straws, page 73

Caesar Salad, page 150

Molten Chocolate Cakes with Cherry Compote, page 83

Hot Pomegranate Grog, page 134